Effective and Caring Leadership

in the Early Years

Education at SAGE

SAGE is a leading international publisher of journals, books, and electronic media for academic, educational, and professional markets.

Our education publishing includes:

- accessible and comprehensive texts for aspiring education professionals and practitioners looking to further their careers through continuing professional development

- inspirational advice and guidance for the classroom

- authoritative state of the art reference from the leading authors in the field

Find out more at: **www.sagepub.co.uk/education**

Effective and Caring Leadership
in the Early Years

Iram Siraj-Blatchford
Elaine Hallet

Los Angeles | London | New Delhi
Singapore | Washington DC

SAGE Publications Ltd
1 Oliver's Yard
55 City Road
London EC1Y 1SP

SAGE Publications Inc.
2455 Teller Road
Thousand Oaks, California 91320

SAGE Publications India Pvt Ltd
B 1/I 1 Mohan Cooperative Industrial Area
Mathura RoadA
New Delhi 110 044

SAGE Publications Asia-Pacific Pte Ltd
3 Church Street
#10–04 Samsung Hub
Singapore 049483

Commissioning editor: Jude Bowen
Assistant editor: Miriam Davey
Production editor: Jeanette Graham
Copyeditor: Carol Lucas
Proofreader: Isabel Kirkwood
Indexer: Avril Ehrlich
Marketing manager: Lorna Patkai
Cover design: Wendy Scott
Typeset by: Dorwyn, Wells, Somerset
Printed by: Replika Press, India

Library of Congress Control Number:
2013937612

British Library Cataloguing in Publication data

A catalogue record for this book is available from the British Library

ISBN 978-1-4462-5534-6
ISBN 978-1-4462-5535-3 (pb)

Contents

List of figures

About the authors

Professor Iram Siraj-Blatchford is an international expert in Early Childhood Education; she has worked with the National College for School Leadership on the National Standards for Leadership in the Early Years and authored an authoritative think-piece on systems leadership. She was the first researcher to write about leadership in centres with proven effective outcomes, from the Effective Provision of Pre-school Education project data. Iram is a leading researcher on pedagogy, curriculum and leadership in the early years. She is committed to research which provides young children, especially those from vulnerable backgrounds, with a fairer start in life. She works as Professor of Early Childhood at the Institute of Education, University of London.

Dr Elaine Hallet is Lecturer in Early Childhood Education at the Institute of Education, University of London. She has a wide experience of working with practitioners, children and families as a teacher, advisory teacher and deputy head teacher and, in further and higher education, as a lecturer, departmental leader and researcher. Elaine has led nationally recognized leadership programmes for graduate Early Years Leaders (EYPs) and children centre leaders (NPQICL) and she leads and teaches a master's level course about leading policy and practice in early childhood services. Elaine has researched foundation degree graduates' Continuous Professional Development through work-based reflective learning and the role of graduate Early Years Leaders in the leadership of learning.

Acknowledgements

This book contains the voices of women early years leaders who were generous enough to allow us to share their effective and caring leadership practices. Among these women leaders are Alison Bishop, Emma Bowery, Alison Evans, Florence E. Fletcher, Amanda Horniman, Anita McKelvey, Maria Meredith, Michelle Palser, Marianna Rapsomanikis and Mags Ratford. Also, thanks to the Early Years Professionals in the LLEaP Project who contributed to our understanding about leadership in settings within the Private, Voluntary and Independent sector and in children's centres, funded by Gloucestershire County Council. We are particularly grateful to practitioners, teachers and leaders in the REPEY and ELEYS Projects who contributed to understandings about leadership in pre-schools and schools, and to the researchers on the EPPE Project, especially Kathy Sylva, Ted Melhuish, Pam Sammons, Brenda Taggart and Laura Manni who contributed to the data collection and analysis of the centres we chose and refer to from the ELEYS Study. Elaine particularly thanks her family for their support during the writing of the book and Iram for initiating the writing project.

Foreword

There has always been a 'right time' for books about leadership. This is *absolutely* the time for a book that adds to our understanding of what constitutes outstanding early years leadership, recognizing that the conduct and behaviour of leaders and their ability to evaluate and develop their skills is instrumental in shifting good settings to become great settings. Here, we have a clearly articulated and carefully researched argument to convince us that 'caring leadership' can create the respectful, affirming yet challenging environment critical to secure consistently high achievement and sustained improvement in pedagogy and outcomes.

The book is fundamentally about building the emotional health of settings in order to establish a culture of caring for and developing people, making the case that these are the settings that will succeed against those that do not know how to care. The content will provoke debate, influence thinking, initiate reflection on practice and, by so doing, will set the direction for further research, whether the reader is an aspirant or practising leader, an academic or simply a 'curious and intrigued individual'. It has both legitimacy and integrity – wherever the readers find themselves on their leadership journey.

As professional leaders, we focus relentlessly on the key components that create 'quality learning and teaching opportunities' for our youngest children and consider how improvements can be made. We recognize our responsibility to define and articulate a narrative around quality. The book strongly suggests that this should include the exploration of *effective and caring leadership* and the potential of such an approach to leadership to impact on the holistic development of children. In the early years, we sometimes walk a fine line between maintaining the caring aspects of leadership (which means avoiding draining people of energy, not curbing their enthusiasm) and addressing improvement imperatives, such as tackling underperformance. We are driven also by the need to secure accountability (which when badly managed can appear threatening and aggressive, and leave people at best disheartened and at worst quietly defeated).

The unique quality of this book is that it invites leaders to reflect on their own behaviours and constructs around leadership while urging consideration of the dispositions and attitudes of highly effective leaders and how these may inspire and influence personal and professional development. It encourages thinking outside the traditional boundaries, beyond the confines of self and setting and into the 'big picture' space of the most effective types of leadership. The international dimension within the book encourages an even broader view of developments across the world lens, widening the horizons of leadership both literally and figuratively. This adds an exciting dimension as we face greater autonomy to make our own decisions in an operating environment that is increasingly relinquishing control from the centre and encouraging responsible local leadership and self-determination.

Case studies representing the authentic voice of practice detail the impact of professional heritage and personal journeys on 'caring leadership' development, enabling those new to the early years sector to gain immediate insight into the multifaceted, complex and integrated nature of early years leadership. For those already engaged in leading within the early years sector, there are familiar echoes of leadership practice, yet with mind-stretching insights to consider and provocative questions to ask and reflect upon.

There is clear ambition from the authors to support the growth of settings that can demonstrate effective and caring leadership illustrated by a passionate commitment to people, wisdom, resourcefulness and a willingness to see reality from a range of perspectives. Ultimately, such leaders recognize that to provide children with the best opportunities to develop, learn and grow, their settings have to be remarkable, joyous places. What is exciting about this book is that it showcases some exceptionally high-performing settings whose outstanding and sustained success has grown out of their commitment to caring leadership at every level of the organization. They are already a quantum leap ahead and are tapping into something that makes them increasingly effective. They are able to work in a climate of overwhelming change by creating an environment in which some of the best leadership behaviours, such as courage, trust and authenticity, can flourish while less helpful attributes may be identified, confronted and vanquished. Such leadership will reflect in happy, creative, compassionate children, ready to make the most of every opportunity and demand still more from their childhood experiences – surely the ultimate measure of learning and care!

Sue Egersdorff, Director for Early Years, National College for
Teaching and Leadership

Pam Mundy, Director for Quality Assurance and Professional
Development, World Class Learning Group

Abbreviations

CCSK	Common Core of Skills and Knowledge for the Children's Workforce
CGFS	Curriculum Guidance for the Foundation Stage
CPD	Continuing Professional Development
DCSF	Department for Children Schools and Families
DFE	Department for Education
DfEE	Department for Education and Employment
DfES	Department for Education and Skills
ECE	Early Childhood Education
ECM	Every Child Matters
ELEYS	Effective Leadership in the Early Years Sector (the ELEYS study, Siraj-Blatchford and Manni, 2007)
ELMS-EY	Effective Leadership and Management Scheme for the Early Years
EPPE	Effective Provision of Pre-school Education (the EPPE project)
EPPSE	Effective Pre-school and Primary Education (3–11) (the EPPSE 3–11 project)
EYFS	Early Years Foundation Stage
EYP	Early Years Professional
EYPS	Early Years Professional Status
EYT	Early Years Teacher
EYTC	Early Years Teaching Centres
GP	General Practitioner
ILP	International Leadership Project
ISSPP	International Successful School Principalship Project
LLEaP	Leadership of Learning in Early Years and Practice (the LLEaP projcct)
NPQH	National Professional Qualification for Head Teachers
NPQICL	National Professional Qualification in Integrated Centre Leadership
NVQ	National Vocational Qualification
Ofsted	Office for Standards in Education
PE	Physical Education

PTA   Parent–Teacher Association
PVI   Private, Voluntary and Independent sector
QTS   Qualified Teacher Status
REPEY   Researching Effective Pedagogy in the Early Years (the REPEY
           study, Siraj-Blatchford et al., 2002)
SIP   School Improvement Plan
SST   Sustained Shared Thinking

Introduction

As the title *Effective and Caring Leadership in the Early Years* implies, this book is about leaders working with young children and their families, educators, teachers, pedagogues, multi-agency professionals and other stakeholders in effective and caring practice. There are other books written about leadership in the early years and about effective leadership, so why is *caring* included in the title along with *effectiveness*?

An ethic of care underpins the nature of work in the field of early childhood and therefore permeates into caring leadership. The ethic of care involves promoting, developing and maintaining caring relationships with staff, children, parents and carers and multi-agency professionals, and it guides professional action. A passion to work with young children is a driver to work and lead in early childhood, in a nurturing and caring way. Children's holistic learning and development is at the heart of caring early years leadership. Effective leadership in the early years should advocate caring as a social principle with a commitment to improving educational, health and social outcomes for children and their families, and for continuing professional learning and development for early years educators, teachers, practitioners and pedagogues.

Leadership is a complex phenomenon. An understanding of leadership in the early years context, its distinctiveness and the characteristics of effective leadership is beginning to unravel through significant research studies as the Effective Leadership in the Early Years Sector study showed (the ELEYS study) (Siraj-Blatchford and Manni, 2007). Effective leadership, particularly by graduate leaders, positively impacts upon children's educational, health, social achievements and well-being. This book builds upon and develops the ELEYS study through a model of Effective and Caring Leadership Practices in Early Childhood in Part 2 of the book.

It is an exciting and challenging time to be writing a book about leadership in the early years as in recent years, there has been extensive reform and change in the field of early childhood both nationally and internationally. Educational policy and workforce reform have raised the status of the early years as an important phase in young children's learning and

1

development, and highlighted the valuable role of adults and leaders who work with young children and families. There has been more awareness of specific leadership practices; for example, pedagogical leadership in enabling children's learning and development; placing learning at the centre of a school, setting or children's centre, and building communities of learning and practice. The practice of collaborative, empowering, distributed and shared leadership supports individual and organizational development, promoting leadership capability and capacity. An understanding of the process of change helps leaders to improve organizations. Relational leadership, the development and sustaining of relationships are essential in effective leadership; collegial, relational, nurturing and caring leadership is emerging as a distinctive characteristic of leadership in the early years.

Organization of the book

The book is intended for existing, recently appointed and aspiring leaders working in the early years sector, studying early years and early childhood studies, and leadership, and for those in teacher training. The chapters in the book intend to highlight issues surrounding leadership for educational and integrated provision in settings, schools and children's centres, aiming to fulfil the need for more clarity about effective and caring leadership practices that make a difference in improving quality provision and outcomes for children and families.

The authors use the terms *early years* and *early childhood* interchangeably, defining 'early childhood' as between birth and 6 years, reflecting national and international frameworks for early learning which range from birth to 6 years, for example, in England, Scotland, Europe and Australia.

The structure of the book in three parts provides a cohesive framework to the topic of effective and caring leadership in early years through:

- theoretical, practical and research informed perspectives

- a model of Effective and Caring Leadership Practices in Early Childhood

- examples of leadership practices in case studies and reflections from early years leaders

- questions for reflection, for existing and aspiring leaders to consider each chapter's leadership topic and their leadership practice

- further reading at the end of each chapter signposts linked reading to extend understanding of themes and concepts discussed in the chapter.

The 11 chapters in the book provide a coherent discussion about effective and caring leadership in the early years; each chapter builds upon the one before but can also be read individually as a themed chapter. In Part 2, there are four sets of paired chapters in the model of Effective and Caring Leadership Practices in Early Childhood, each leadership theme has two chapters about associated leadership practices. The chapters can be read individually or as a pair of chapters.

Part 1: Leadership in early childhood

Chapter 1, 'The early years context': This chapter provides a context for effective and caring leadership in early childhood by exploring the evolving leadership landscape in the early years sector, discussing professional learning opportunities for leadership development, examining the relationship between leadership and management, and exploring the distinctiveness of leadership in the early years, referring to the ethic of care within early childhood, inclusive leadership, women as leaders and distributed shared leadership within integrated practice. Leadership in early years settings, schools and children's centres has been recognized as significant in raising standards and increasing the quality of educational, health and social outcomes for children.

Chapter 2, 'The research context', examines research studies about leadership in early childhood. The research studies Researching Effective Pedagogy in the Early Years (the REPEY study), Effective Leadership in the Early Years Sector (the ELEYS study) and Leadership of Learning in Early Years Practice (the LLEaP project) are discussed, describing the design, research methodology and key findings of the studies, and identifying requirements, characteristics and practices for effective and caring leadership in early childhood.

Part 2: Effective early childhood leadership

In the **'Introduction'** a model of Effective and Caring Leadership Practices in Early Childhood, which forms Part 2 of the book, is introduced. The four leadership themes, *directional leadership, collaborative leadership, empowering leadership* and *pedagogical leadership*, and eight leadership practices, *developing a shared vision, effective communication, promoting a team culture, promoting parental collaboration, promoting agency in others, leading the process of change, leading learning* and *reflective learning*, provide a framework for early childhood leaders to understand further the phenomenon of early years leadership.

In **Chapter 3, 'Directional leadership: developing a shared vision'**, the theme of *directional leadership* in effective and caring leadership is defined and the leadership practice of *developing a shared vision* explored. The ability of a leader to develop and articulate a shared vision is central in directional leadership, providing a purposeful pathway for policy, provision and practice within the early years setting, children's centre or school. The chapter discusses the development and articulation of vision within directional leadership, considers an example of directional leadership practice and provides opportunity to reflect upon directional leadership and developing a shared vision.

Chapter 4, 'Directional leadership: effective communication': the leadership practice of *effective communication* within the *directional leadership* theme in effective and caring leadership in the early years is discussed in this chapter. Leaders' ability to communicate effectively is clearly linked to the articulation of vision to all stakeholders, including children, influencing others and promoting consistency in policy, provision and practice. The chapter explores effective communication in directional leadership, considers the role of active listening in effective communication, examines emotional intelligence within leadership and provides opportunity to reflect upon effective communication in directional leadership.

In **Chapter 5, 'Collaborative leadership: promoting a team culture',** the theme of *collaborative leadership* in effective and caring leadership is defined and the leadership practice of *promoting a team culture* explored. The chapter highlights the importance of the promotion of a team culture, with an understanding that successful settings, schools and children's centres rely upon the forging and sustaining of relationships within and beyond the organization. There is opportunity for reflection about collaborative leadership, experiencing a team culture and working in a team, through examples of leadership practice and reflective questions.

In **Chapter 6, 'Collaborative leadership: promoting parental collaboration',** the leadership practice of *promoting parental collaboration* within the *collaborative leadership* theme in effective and caring leadership in the early years is discussed. The importance for leaders to promote collaborative involvement and work in partnership with parents in their child's early education, at home, at transition, and in early years settings, children's centres and schools is discussed and illustrated through examples of leadership practice. There is opportunity to reflect upon working with parents and leading parental involvement in a collaborative way.

In **Chapter 7, 'Empowering leadership: promoting agency in others',** the theme *empowering leadership* in effective and caring leadership in the early years is defined and the leadership practice of *promoting agency in others* through transformational leadership explored. A leader's ability to influence and empower others to lead is a central leadership practice. Through distributed, shared and transformative leadership, this leadership practice builds individual leadership capability and capacity within an organization and for its future development. There is opportunity for reflection about empowering leadership and promoting agency in others through examples of practice and reflective questions.

In **Chapter 8, 'Empowering leadership: the process of change'**, the leadership practice of *leading the process of change* within the *empowering leadership* theme in effective and caring leadership in the early years is explored. One of the key skills required by those leading settings, schools, centres and services is the ability to understand the process of change, to lead, implement and sustain change; change which is both internally and externally motivated and mandated. In the current context of change in the early years sector, which has brought increasing attention and accountability to those in positions of leadership, the ability to lead change within an organization is important. This chapter considers the process of change for organizational improvement, explores catalytic leadership in leading change and discusses system leadership in school improvement. There is opportunity for reflection about empowering leadership and leading the change through examples of practice and reflective questions.

In **Chapter 9, 'Pedagogical leadership: leading learning'**, the theme *pedagogical leadership* in effective and caring leadership in the early years is defined and the leadership practice of *leading learning* in its broadest sense is explored, situating learning at the centre of an organization. The chapter defines pedagogy and pedagogical leadership, examines pedagogical leadership and its contribution to quality of provision, pedagogy and practice, and the development and role of graduate pedagogical leaders, and considers learning communities of practice. There is opportunity for reflection about pedagogical leadership and leading learning through examples of practice and reflective questions.

In **Chapter 10, 'Pedagogical leadership: leading reflective learning'**, the leadership practice of *leading reflective learning* within the *pedagogical leadership* theme in effective and caring leadership in the early years is explored. The chapter discusses the generally accepted view of the importance of promoting staff's continuing professional learning and development through reflective practice and collaborative dialogue. This chapter considers the relationship between continuing professional learning and development for quality of provision, explores how pedagogical leaders can provide opportunities for reflective dialogue and learning, and examines approaches to monitoring practice and to giving feedback and signposting for further development of practice. There is opportunity for reflection about pedagogical leadership and leading reflective learning through examples of practice and reflective questions.

Part 3: Reflective leadership

Chapter 11, 'Leadership stories', is the concluding chapter. Effective and caring leadership practices are illustrated and demonstrated through lived experiences of leadership through narrative exploration. Three early years leaders share their autobiographical reflective stories of their leadership journeys, understandings of their identity as leaders and their leadership styles and practices. Their stories demonstrate the leadership themes and practices of directional, collaborative, empowering and pedagogical leadership in the model of Effective and Caring Leadership Practices in Early Childhood discussed earlier in the book. There is opportunity for existing and aspiring leaders to illustrate and reflect upon their leadership story-of-experience.

Part 1

Leadership in early childhood

Introduction

The two chapters in Part 1 provide a contextual overview of leadership within early childhood and a theoretical base from academic literature and significant research studies. Evidence from literature and research demonstrates the importance of leadership in raising standards of learning and educational outcomes for children. Leadership is a complex phenomenon and the complexity and distinctiveness of leadership within early years contexts is beginning to unravel. Reference to other writers in the field and the authors' own research forms the discussion about leadership in early childhood in Part 1 and is a contextual base for subsequent chapters in the book.

Leadership in the early years is like a river flowing through an emerging leadership landscape of hills and valleys. The discussion includes national and international perspectives, placing early childhood leadership within a global map of constructs and understanding around the distinctiveness of leadership in the early years. The discussion explores how research has informed and shaped our understanding about early years leaders' behaviour and practices. Both effective and caring leadership practices are defined and discussed within a contextual framework of the early years sector within Part 1 of the book, forming smaller tributary rivers and streams for further discussion and reflection in Part 2.

1

Leadership in early childhood: the early years context

Chapter overview

Leadership in early years settings, schools and children's centres has been recognized as significant in raising standards and increasing the quality of educational, health and social outcomes for children. Effective and caring leadership is an evolving area of importance in developing quality provision for young children and families. This chapter provides a discussion about the evolving leadership landscape and the distinctiveness of leadership within the early years context.

This chapter will:

- explore the evolving leadership landscape in the early years sector
- discuss professional learning opportunities for leadership development
- examine the relationship between leadership and management
- consider the distinctiveness of leadership in the early years.

The evolving leadership landscape

Leadership is a complex phenomenon with numerous definitions to understand the concept of leadership and being a leader. Terms such as leadership, leading and leaders are often used interchangeably. In essence, leadership is portrayed as a purposeful and positive activity (Fitzgerald and Gunter, 2008). The relationship between effective educational leadership, teacher leadership and school leadership for school improvement and positive educational outcomes for children and young people has been evidenced (Bush et al., 2010). For example, leadership practices that directly linked with and support improved outcomes for students in Queensland, Australia, were described by Lingard et al. (2003) as productive leadership. Starratt (2003) argues that a shift in focus from solo leadership of an organization to a focus on leadership of learning and shared distributed leadership, placing learners at the centre of the organization, links learning, leaders and leadership.

An understanding of leadership within the wider context of early years settings and children's centres is evolving, as is the impact upon educational, health, social and well-being outcomes for children (Rodd, 2013; Siraj-Blatchford and Manni, 2007; Siraj-Blatchford et al., 2002). The emerging understanding points to leadership being a relational and communal concept where all can be a leader, engage in leadership, benefit from leadership and exercise power and individual agency when leadership is distributed and shared (Fitzgerald and Gunter, 2008). Leadership is transformative and empowering for individuals; Greenleaf (2003: 15) highlights that 'true leadership emerges from those whose primary motivation is a desire to help others'.

A global understanding of leadership in early childhood and its relationship to professionalism is developing from a 'ground up' perspective (Dalli, 2008). The nationally recognized status and pedagogical leadership role of the graduate Early Years Professional (EYP) in England, linked leadership with the professionalization and raising the status of the early years workforce. Duhn (2011: 141) views professionalism and leadership as closely interlinked with the learning self. Ellsworth (2005) theorizes the learning self as movement and experiences, the professional and personal self reshaping each other in an ongoing process of professional 'knowledge in the making'. Leadership and learning reshapes leadership and is an aspect of professionalism.

Theories of leadership, trait, behavioural, situational and transformational theories have informed understanding of leadership (Whalley, 2011a). There are cultural and contextual aspects that influence leadership style and practices. The International Successful School Principalship Project (ISSPP) (Moos et al., 2008) aimed to identify successful school leadership practices in different geographical locations and with pupils from different socio-economic backgrounds. The construct of 'success' applied to school leadership in the project was contextualized and relational, referring to multiple perspectives within the case study schools. In most schools, the principal set the direction for the school. In some schools, the direction was formulated by the principal while in other schools the direction was the product of dialogue and shared sense and knowledge making.

In the Scandinavian context, democratic principles were applied to school leadership. In Sweden, many schools formed teacher teams and distributed both responsibility and decision-making to them. Principals in Tasmania, Australia, strove for a culture of collegiality and collaboration in which the principals set directions. The Chinese school system has a hierarchy of leaders and has strong top-down communities. Decisions and policy were made at district level and implemented in a top-down way; by managers at lower levels and then in a similar way in Chinese schools. A focus on performance standards in New York state schools in the USA, stimulated collaborative dialogue and shared learning to monitor progress. Leadership was distributed to teacher teams for shared planning and decision-making. In the UK, principals developed vision for improving pupils' achievement. They set vision and direction for their school and education but also delegated tasks and responsibility for implementing those visions to teachers' teams.

International developments within early childhood demonstrate the changing nature of early years services in several parts of the world and the evolving nature and understanding of leadership. While there are con-textual differences between countries, there is renewed interest in the early years phase of children's learning and development and the affirmation of the importance of this stage of education as a major factor propelling change in service and provision (Chan and Mellor, 2002).

Leaders often take up leadership roles without training (Aubrey, 2011) and, internationally, qualifications vary. Practitioners undertaking early childhood leadership in Australia, New Zealand and Europe hold different qualifications, including diploma, degree, master's degree and teaching qualifications. In Australia the majority of practitioners working in early childhood services are qualified teachers (Jonsdottir and Hard, 2009). In New Zealand an integrated service of education and care is delivered in early childhood centres by teachers (Dalli, 2008). Few practitioners have specific qualifications in leadership, although many head teachers in Iceland have a diploma in leadership from a one-year graduate study and some have a master's degree (Jonsdottir and Hard, 2009). The selection of terms used in early childhood services in Europe, listed in Figure 1.1, shows the range of job titles used to describe the role of practitioners who work with young children from birth to 7 years (Oberhuemer et al., 2010).

At a glance the term 'leader' is missing from the plethora of names, although the words pedagogue, teacher, professional are common terminology. The job title names, nursery nurse, teaching assistant, teacher, Early Years Professional and Early Years Practitioner used in England add to confusion about roles and responsibilities for those working in the early years sector. In the *Foundations for Quality* report about early education and childcare qualifications (DfE, 2012: 46), Nutbrown proposed a new set of job titles for qualified staff within the workforce in England: early years practitioner (level 3), senior early years practitioner (level 4 and above), Early Years Professional (graduate with Early Year Professional Status – EYPS) and Early Years Teacher (graduate with Qualified Teacher Status – QTS). Their pedagogical leadership role identified:

early years practitioners leading practice within a room, senior early years practitioners leading practice across a number of rooms, Early Years Professionals (EYPs) leading practice across a setting and qualified Early Years Teachers (EYTs) providing overall pedagogical leadership for a setting, all working directly with children and families. The range of Early Years Practitioners in Nutbrown's proposal of job roles have leadership responsibility in supporting and supervising unqualified or less qualified staff. In the Truss Report, *More Great Childcare* (DfE, 2013), the job title 'early years educator' is used for practitioners qualified to level 3, and the term 'Early Years Teacher' is used for graduate leaders, replacing the proposed titles by Nutbrown. The new job titles change the role emphasis from practice to education.

Country	Job title
Austria	Kindergarten pedagogue
Belgium	Social pedagogy professional
	Infant-toddler professional
Czech Republic	Teacher
Denmark	Pedagogue
France	Pre-primary teacher
Ireland	Primary school teacher
	Basic practitioner in early childhood/care
	Intermediate practitioner in early childhood/care
	Experienced practitioner in early childhood/care
	Advanced practitioner in early childhood/care
	Expert practitioner in early childhood/care
Italy	Early childhood education teacher
	Assistant in community work with young children
	Educator
	Integration teacher
Romania	Pre-primary and primary school professional
Spain	Teacher in early childhood education
	Senior specialist in early childhood education
Sweden	Teacher of young children

Figure 1.1 European early childhood job titles

The Effective Pre-school Provision in Education (EPPE) research study in England found higher-quality provision and children's cognitive outcomes in pre-schools led by staff with graduate degree qualifications. Less qualified staff benefited from working with staff with higher qualifications (Oberhuemer et al., 2010). Research studies in America (Barnett, 2004) concerning the relationship between the qualifications of staff and quality of early years services found that the education levels of staff, together with a specialist professional qualification in Early Childhood Education, predict both the qualities of interactions between teacher and child, and children's learning and development.

Government reform proposals in England within the Truss Report (DfE, 2013) recognize the contribution of graduate early years leaders who are EYPs in helping to improve the quality of education but whose public status is low. The government wants to introduce more graduates in the early years. Early Years Professionals and EYTs have a pedagogical leadership role. Early Years Teachers will be introduced to build on the EYPS programme, and existing EYPs will be recognized as EYTs, specialists in early childhood development. Early Years Teachers will be seen as equivalent to QTS. As Nutbrown (2013) in her response to the Truss Report argues, this will bring inequality of status and pay for Early Years Teachers with QTS and those without. The introduction of the terms 'Early Years Educator' and 'Early Years Teacher' in the Truss Report (DfE, 2013) highlights the government's emphasis on children's education, learning and graduate pedagogical leadership.

Similarly, Early Years Teaching Centres (EYTC) promote a regional focus on teaching, learning and the leadership for learning. These centres provide effective pedagogical leadership through a combination of training, support and demonstrating outstanding practice. There is evidence to show (Pen Green, 2012) that this model of professional learning through communities of practice is improving children's outcomes both in the setting and within the EYTC's region.

Leadership development in the early years

Leadership has been taking place with nursery and infant schools in England for many years by head and deputy head teachers in nursery schools and by teachers in nursery classes and units (Hallet, 2013a). In these contexts, leadership seemed to be the domain of educational institutions such as schools. Leadership was little acknowledged in early years settings where care and education took place, for example, in Sure Start children's centres and in early years settings in the Private, Voluntary and Independent sector (PVI) such as in playgroups, pre-schools, crèches, full daycare and sessional provision. Many teachers and practitioners, particularly women, who were also leaders, preferred to recognize their teaching role rather than their leadership role of leading people, resources and curriculum (Rodd, 2013). Although leadership in the early years sector was happening, it seems to have gone unrecognized (Bennis and Nanus, 1997) until more recently.

The introduction of leadership programmes for leaders of practice – the Early Years Professional Status training programme, the National Professional Qualification in Integrated Centre Leadership (NPQICL) for integrated centre leaders in children's centres and the National Professional Qualification for Head Teachers (NPQH) – has provided opportunities for practitioners and teachers to access nationally recognized leadership training through higher education (CWDC, 2008; NC, 2010). One of the main findings from the EPPE project (Sylva et al., 2010) and the associated Researching Effective Pedagogy in the Early Years (REPEY) study (Siraj-Blatchford et al., 2002) was that settings with higher-quality scores were those where staff had higher qualifications (Cottle and Alexander, 2012). The importance of leadership learning throughout a career is recognized for developing leadership sustainability. School systems in Australia have developed a leadership continuum framework that supports the leadership journey from aspirations through to beginning in leadership roles, consolidation and growth, high achievement in the role and transitions to other roles (Anderson et al., 2007). In England, The National College for Teaching and Leadership, formerly the National College for School Leadership, provides professional development programmes for aspiring leaders and those in middle leadership.

The government's Children's Workforce Strategy (DfES, 2005a) highlighted the need to develop a more highly qualified workforce, particularly in the PVI sector. The introduction of the graduate leadership training programme, EYPS and the EYP role as a leader of practice for those working in the PVI sector aimed to address this issue (CWDC, 2008). Those working in the early years sector are regarded as the most underpaid with least status within the public sector (Miller and Cable, 2008). Government funding from the Transformation and Graduate Leader Funds (2006–11) provided financial access for many practitioners, particularly women, to higher education, furthering their qualifications and career opportunities (DFE, 2011). Evidence from the national longitudinal study of graduate leadership training (EYPS) demonstrates that graduate leadership training impacts upon leaders' practice, particularly those in the early stages of their career (Hadfield et al., 2011).

Leadership and management

Early years settings, schools, children's centres and their leaders are very diverse in character, as well as in quality and effectiveness. They are charged with proactively leading and managing related areas of care, health and family support, and integrating these with education, managing budgets and reporting information (Siraj-Blatchford and Manni, 2007). They also need effectively to manage, deploy and develop staff with different professional perspectives and associated qualifications as well as with varying levels of experience and exposure to professional training (Siraj-Blatchford and Manni, 2007). Accompanying this there is public demand for greater accountability and pressure to achieve excellence in service and health, educational and social outcomes for children (Aubrey, 2011).

The multifaceted aspects of leadership and management can merge into one role; the terms are used interchangeably in the early years sector but frequently there is an emphasis on being a manager, rather than a leader. Siraj-Blatchford and Manni (2007: 25) in the *Effective Leadership in the Early Years Sector (The ELEYS Study)*, found it was important to strike a balance in leading and managing a setting, as the administrative role can take precedence over leading teaching and learning.

In the following case study from the LLEaP project, the early years leader in a private day nursery reflects upon leadership and management roles within the nursery's senior team.

Case study: Leader's reflection – leading and managing a nursery

The nursery owner, Lisa, reflects about the management and leadership of her small nursery which is situated in the downstairs of her large Victorian house:

> The nursery leadership and management team consists of me as the owner, Sue the nursery manager and Deena the deputy manager. There are administrative, financial and curriculum tasks; Sue and Deena share these between them. Deena went on a graduate leadership training course, and came back with lots of ideas and theories about how children learn and develop. As the Toddler Room Leader, she tried out new ideas and activities with the children; she involved and discussed what she was doing with the practitioners in the Toddler Room. Deena was beginning to take a leadership role in curriculum and learning within the nursery; staff began to ask her advice for activities to do with children. As deputy manager, Deena also spent time in administrative tasks such as arranging staff rotas, collecting dinner and trip monies, ordering resources, all of which took her away from working with children.
>
> We have weekly management team meetings. We discussed the influence of Deena's developing specialized knowledge upon nursery provision and practitioners' practice. We want to allow time for Deena to use her developing expertise more. To do this we agreed

(Continues)

(Continued)

for Deena and Sue to have two distinct roles, one with more emphasis on curriculum leadership and the other with emphasis on
administrative and financial tasks of a manager's role. They now
have specific roles, new job titles and job descriptions to reflect the
work they do in the nursery. Deena has a designated role as Curriculum Leader and Sue has a designated role as Nursery Manager.
This allows them to work together in a defined and focused way in
two parallel roles. Deena has time to lead the curriculum for children's
learning and development, as a room leader, and for whole-setting
curriculum development through leading staff meetings, mentoring
and supporting practitioners in their work with young children and
families. Sue has time to carry out administrative and financial tasks
for the day-to-day smooth running of the nursery; undertaking
budgetary monitoring and reporting to others such as the management committee and outside agencies like Ofsted [Office for
Standards in Education]. These two parallel but complementary
roles allow for effective leadership and management of the nursery.

The case study demonstrates an organizational restructuring for leadership
activity. Outstanding leadership has invariably emerged as a key
characteristic of outstanding schools and pre-school provision (Ofsted,
2003; Sylva et al., 2010). There is widespread recognition that leadership is
second only to classroom practice in terms of impact on school and
children's outcomes (Bush et al., 2010). Strong primary and secondary
leadership and management are key factors in effective schools (Ofsted,
2003b). The contribution of educational leadership for improving
organizational performance, raising achievement and quality of provision
(Muijs et al., 2004; Sylva et al., 2010) is influencing leadership in early
years settings, and its distinctiveness is now explored.

Distinctive leadership in the early years

Leadership has several traits and attributes to unravel and make sense of
(Friedman, 2007). The concept of leadership has developed from
educational models of leadership found in schools, a hierarchical concept
of leadership being associated with a sole owner, a single person with
authority to lead, undertake and carry out tasks alone (Rodd, 2013) being
a charismatic leader who others follow resonates with this view. Weber
(1968: 241) explains that a person with 'charisma' has a certain quality of
individual personality that is considered as extraordinary, endowed with
exceptional powers or qualities. On the basis of these personality qualities,
the individual concerned is treated as a 'leader'.

However, this well-established view of leadership is changing. The view of leadership, as collaborative, relational and interdependent, rather than hierarchical, is emerging from within the early years sector (McDowall Clark and Murray, 2012; Rodd, 2013). Leadership within the early years sector concerns relational leadership, groups of people collaboratively working together to complete tasks and goals rather than being the work of one leader (Siraj-Blatchford and Manni, 2007). Rodd (2013) defines leaders working in early childhood as people who can influence the behaviours of others to achieve a goal or planned outcome. They possess a set of qualities and skills which combine an ability to influence and motivate others to do what the leader wants because they want to do it. They do this by using personal qualities which promote feelings of trust, motivation and security. Leaders are responsible for developing and articulating a shared vision, setting and clarifying goals, roles and responsibilities, collecting information and planning, making decisions and involving members of the group by communicating, encouraging and acknowledging commitment and contribution. Leadership concerns creating the conditions in which all members of the organization can give their best in a climate of commitment, reflection and challenge. Leadership is a process for personal and professional learning and development; organizational change and improvement.

The graduate early years leader (EYP, EYT) as a leader of practice (Whalley, 2011b) places leadership as an important factor in early years settings in the PVI sector. McDowall Clark and Murray (2012) discuss perspectives of early years leadership, recognizing leadership can come from anywhere within the organization, particularly if the setting is a 'leaderful community' (Raelin, 2003: 44) of shared and distributed leadership. Their paradigm of 'leadership within' defines a new concept of early years leadership as collective, group based, participatory and shared. 'It is non-hierarchical, flexible and responsive enabling leadership to emerge at any level of the organization wherever the appropriate knowledge and expertise or initiative occurs and with the ability to identify and act on challenges and opportunities' (McDowall Clark and Murray, 2012: 12). The term 'leadership within' illustrates leadership found in the non-hierarchical nature of many small early years settings in the PVI sector, led by play leaders, room leaders, nursery managers and management committees; in comparison to the hierarchical nature of the composition of school leadership teams of head teacher, deputy head teacher, assistant head teacher, phase leaders, subject leaders and curriculum coordinators. A similar inclusive and democratic leadership style was found in the LLEaP project (Hallet and Roberts-Holmes, 2010). The Nutbrown Review (DfE, 2012) regards leadership as inclusive and the responsibility of all who work in schools, settings and children's centres. This view develops sustainable leadership and supports the model of system leadership across a range of schools, children's centres and early years settings, currently being developed in the Foundation Years (NC, 2012). The influence of gender upon inclusive leadership and the distinctiveness of women as leaders are now explored.

Inclusive leadership

The composition of the early education and childcare workforce is predominantly women, averaging between 98 and 99 per cent depending on setting type. Working with children and particularly young children is widely regarded as 'women's work' (Nutbrown, 2012: 41). There are issues around the lack of men working in the sector and also the under-representation of black and minority ethnic groups within the workforce (Nutbrown, 2012) as well as the representation of women in leadership roles. There are more men working as teachers in primary schools, usually with older children, than with very young children in the Foundation Years (birth to 5 years of age) and fewer with babies and young children under 3 years of age. The sensitivities about child abuse and perceptions of men working with children may mean men meet with prejudice and mistrust, resulting in fewer men becoming early years or infant teachers, nursery nurses, early years practitioners and teaching assistants (Cushman, 2005). The widely held view that working in early education and childcare is low status and underpaid (Nutbrown, 2012; Vincent and Braun, 2010) affects diverse recruitment into the workforce.

The demographics of the workforce are reflected in leadership within the early years sector. Internationally, the only area of education where most leaders are women is in early years provision (Lumby and Coleman, 2007). There is a tendency for men working in areas of female-dominated work to gain promotion (Lumby and Coleman, 2007) and become leaders within, and of, schools, settings, children's centres, private daycare organizations and children's services. Men entering into primary teaching in England are likely to reach a senior post. In nursery and the primary sector, 16 per cent of primary teachers are male teachers, yet 38 per cent of head teachers are men (DfES, 2004a). Cameron (2001: 439), in a review of literature about men working in childcare in the UK, USA, Australia and Scandinavia, found that men do well financially and access work opportunities when they do 'women's work'.

There are varied social and cultural reasons for this gender inbalance. In a review of literature on women leading at work (Coleman, 2008), gender stereotypes relating to leadership and assumptions about family responsibilities were an integral component of the stereotypes relating to gender and leadership. Coleman summarizes barriers to career progression for women as:

- a masculine work culture, particularly at senior levels

- gender stereotypes which cast men as leaders, women as supporters and nurturers and therefore 'outsiders' as leaders

- the actual and perceived impact of family responsibilities on women's ability to work.

Stereotypical views and assumptions about leadership and who become leaders, inform the gender discourse about leadership. Weyer (2007), in reviewing the persistence of the glass ceiling of leadership for women, identifies the cultural view that leadership is a task and requires behaviours that are deemed masculine. Miller (2006) identifies the stereotype within our culture of men with more agentic leadership behaviour and women with more nurturing and supportive, communal roles. Shakeshaft (1987), in a gendered analysis of educational leadership and management, suggests that women's leadership style tends to be more democratic and participatory, encouraging inclusiveness and holding a broader view of the curriculum. McDowall and Murray (2012) note that an ethic of care (Osgood, 2004) underpins the nature of work in the early years and is a defining characteristic that permeates caring leadership. However, Blackmore (1999) suggests that men's public admittance to feminine leadership qualities continues to maintain their advantage in leadership.

Leadership behaviours and qualities that are stereotypically female or male, do not exclude the other gender from sharing these. Effective leaders should share qualities that are both stereotypically feminine and masculine (Gilligan, 1982) and knowingly use appropriate leadership behaviours for a particular situation and context. Both women and men head teachers aspire to a democratic, nurturing feminine leadership style (Lumby and Coleman, 2007) particularly in the early years sector. Leaders should combine both affective (feminine) and rational (male) ways of working, and use a broad range of qualities and behaviours (McDowall and Murray, 2012).

There is an absence of gender from theories of leadership (Runte and Miles, 2006). Standpoint theory holds the view that women have a particular view of the world and of life because of their experience as women, which is bound to differ from that of men (Coleman, 2011). There is emerging understanding of leadership behaviours and qualities of women as leaders. Chrisholm (2001: 398) refers to 'maternal feminism' with women harnessing experience and qualities from motherhood, asserting a version of the 'strong woman' in their leadership style, behaviour and qualities, being nurturing, democratic and assertive. This attitude begins to challenge the traditional view of leadership and reconceptualizes leadership for diversity of leaders. Through graduate and postgraduate leadership programmes there are many women leaders in the early years sector as children centre leaders, leaders in integrated practice in children's services, and in nurseries, settings and schools. Through higher education the 'invisible workforce' of women traditionally working in supportive roles in education, health and social services are now in the forefront of leading provision, services and practice (Hallet, 2013a: 10). Their shared and distributed style of leadership is now discussed within the value base of an ethic of care.

Caring leadership

The context for care and education and caring leadership in the delivery of multidisciplinary children's services in England developed from the Rumbold Report, Starting with Quality (DES, 1990), highlighting inequality of provision for 3- and 4-year olds within early years settings and schools in the maintained and PVI sectors. The report recommended the delivery of care integrated with education, and the concept of 'educare' in the delivery of multi-agency services was introduced (MacLeod-Brudenell, 2008). The Rumbold Report recommended a higher qualified workforce with multidisciplinary knowledge and understanding for working with young children and families. The introduction of undergraduate degrees in early childhood studies, incorporating health, social and educational perspectives in working with children and families, promoted a holistic and integrated way of working (DES, 1990).

The introduction of the Labour government's strategy *Every Child Matters: Change for Children* (DfES, 2004b) set out strategic plans for bringing together all services with responsibility for children, young people and families under one coherent national framework through a social justice agenda of equalizing and optimizing later life chances (Knowles, 2009). The more recent government review of provision furthers holistic multi-agency approach to service delivery; the Marmot Review (Marmot, 2010), of health inequalities identified a complex interaction of many factors – housing, financial, education and social – which are largely preventable, and there is a strong social justice and economic case for addressing health inequalities (Marmot, 2010). The Allen Review (Allen, 2011: xi) furthers holistic delivery of services for young children and families through early intervention policies and programmes to identify multi-agency support for children aged from birth to 3 years which help give them the 'social and emotional bedrock they need to reach their full potential'. The Munro Review of child protection and safeguarding children endorses Sure Start children's centres and the health visitor service in delivering early intervention programmes and in reporting early intervention outcomes (Munro, 2010). The Field Review (2010: 6) examined poverty and its impact upon children's life changes, recommending greater prominence be given to the earliest years in life, from pregnancy to the age of 5, adopting the term 'Foundation Years', to increase understanding of how babies and young children develop healthily, and recommending support for children and parents in the early years, and to ensure that child development and services during those early years are well understood. The Tickell Review (2011: 4) of early educational provision in the Early Years Foundation Stage (EYFS) curriculum recommended further inclusion of the holistic nature of children's learning and development.

Within this landscape of review and policy development there is a need for caring and effective leadership of children's services, children's centres, early years settings and schools. An ethic of care underpins practitioners' and leaders' work with young children and families (Osgood, 2006), contributing to caring leadership practice in the early years sector. The ethic of care involves developing and maintaining caring relationships with children, parents and carers, and multi-agency professionals, which guides professional action, placing the welfare, interests and outcomes for children at the centre of the service. A passion to work with young children is a driver to work and lead in early childhood in a nurturing and caring way (Hallet, 2013b). Leadership in the early years should advocate caring as a social principle (McDowall Clark and Murray, 2012) with a commitment to improving educational, health and social outcomes for children. Children's holistic learning and development is at the heart of caring leadership, which includes leading multi-agency teams in integrated practice through distributed and shared leadership. Caring leadership requires a leadership style of distributed and shared leadership. This approach to leadership is now discussed within the context of Sure Start children's centres.

Distributed and shared leadership

SureStart children's centres bring together services for children under 5 and their families, offering services that integrate health, childcare, education, parent involvement, family support and employment services, and 'children's centres that provide more and better integrated services are improving outcomes for children' (DCSF, 2007: 3). The leaders of children's centres have the responsibility of leading a diverse range of multi-professional integrated service delivery. Practitioners working in children's centres are from a range of different professional backgrounds offering a range of services to support parents and children in the Foundation Years; for example, a midwife, employment adviser, health visitor, health carer, speech and language therapist, social worker, family support, nursery nurse. The range of services offered may include childcare, healthy eating progammes, midwife appointments, General Practitioner (GP) medical appointments, outreach family support, early intervention programmes, play-and-stay sessions, baby massage sessions, fathers' group, debt advice and job centre information.

Children's centre services are distinct owing to the collaboration and cooperation of different professional groups and agencies working together in integrated practice in providing services for children, parents and families (DCSF, 2007). The leadership and coordination of the complex range of services is challenging for leaders of children's centres (Lord et al., 2011). The expansion of integrated multi-agency services for young children and families has affected leadership roles, definitions and expectations placed upon leaders working in the early years sector (Pugh, 2006). Leading integrated practice has led to change in the ways leadership is viewed in early years settings, from a model of the head of centre being the only leader, to a model of distributed and shared leadership within and across the centre's services. It is unrealistic for a centre leader to be knowledgeable about all services. The centre leader requires a range of strategies to promote the best outcomes for children, to lead across professional boundaries and distribute leadership among the whole staff team (Duffy and Marshall, 2007). Integrated practice requires leadership approaches, such as distributed and sustainable leadership, which offer opportunities for leadership to be distributed and shared among teams. The centre leader has a strategic role for the services the centre provides, promotes the centre's vision, developed with the whole staff team, is able to trust the specialized knowledge and expertise of multi-professional teams and team leaders, and is able to support as appropriate and challenge staff when necessary (Duffy and Marshall, 2007) in a caring and effective way.

 Summary

This chapter has provided a context for effective and caring leadership in early childhood by exploring the evolving leadership landscape in the early years sector; discussing professional learning opportunities for leadership development; examining the relationship between leadership and management; and exploring the distinctiveness of leadership in the early years referring to the ethic of care within early childhood, inclusively of leadership, women as leaders and distributed shared leadership within integrated practice.

 The next chapter considers research studies about leadership in early childhood, highlighting contextual requirements, characteristics and leadership practices for effective early years settings, children's centres and schools.

Further reading

Bloch, M.N. (2008) 'Gender, work, and child care: crossing borders in the life and work of Sally Lubeck', *Journal of Early Childhood Research*, 6(1): 31–45.
   The focus of this journal article is on the themes of gender, work and childcare as addressed in Sally Lubeck's work in the USA.
Coleman, M. (2011) *Women at the Top: Challenges, Choice and Change*. Basingstoke: Palgrave Macmillan.
   This book provides a broad perspective of women, work and leadership through authentic women's voices.
Miller, L. and Cable, C. (eds) (2011) *Professionalization, Leadership and Management in the Early Years*. London: Sage.
   This book examines the interest in and development of professionalism and

leadership in early childhood, providing reflective insights.

Moyles, J. (2001) 'Passion, paradox and professionalism in early years education', *Early Years*, 21(2): 81–95.

This journal article explores the notion of a passionate early years workforce.

Siraj-Blatchford, I., Clarke, K. and Needham, M. (eds) (2007) *The Team around the Child: Multi-agency Working in the Early Years*. Stoke-on-Trent: Trentham Books.

This book has a multi-agency focus and underpins theoretical perspectives for integrated practice and distributed leadership.

2

Leadership in early childhood: the research context

Chapter overview

In this chapter, research studies about leadership in early childhood are examined, highlighting important leadership requirements, characteristics and practices for effective and caring leadership in early years settings, children's centres and schools. The following studies are discussed; Researching Effective Pedagogy in the Early Years (the REPEY study), the Effective Leadership in the Early Years Sector (the ELEYS study) and the Leadership of Learning in Early Years Practice (the LLEaP project).

This chapter will:

- describe the design, research methodology and key findings of three research studies about leadership in the early years
- identify requirements, characteristics and practices for effective and caring leadership in early childhood.

Researching Effective Pedagogy in the Early Years (REPEY study)

The REPEY study (Siraj-Blatchford et al., 2002) was a sister study to the Effective Provision of Pre-school Education (EPPE) project (Sylva et al., 2010), a longitudinal study that assessed the attainment and development of children followed from the age of 3 until the end of Key Stage 1, when the children were 7 years of age. Over 3,000 children were recruited to the study during 1997–99 from 141 pre-school centres, that is, nursery schools, nursery classes and playgroups.

The early years settings in the EPPE project were selected from a random sample of the six main forms of pre-school provision in five regions in England. The study aimed for 20–25 children to be randomly sampled in each pre-school centre when they entered, and their progress was followed through to the end of Key Stage 1. Both qualitative and quantitative methods were used to explore the effects of the pre-school experience on children's cognitive attainment and social/behavioural development at entry to school and any continuing effects on such outcomes up to 7 years of age. In addition to the effects of pre-school experience, the EPPE study investigated the contribution to children's development of individual child and family characteristics, such as gender, family size, parental education and employment.

The REPEY study was based on in-depth case studies exploring the pedagogical practices observed and reported occurring in 12 early years settings selected from the original 141 EPPE settings. The addition of two reception classes, in the REPEY study, was to ensure that all major types of early years group care and educational settings were represented. These early years settings represented moderate (slightly above average) to effective (well above average) settings based upon both cognitive and social/ behavioural child outcomes. All of the settings elected for the case studies demonstrate a range of practices; all of them demonstrate some above average outcome(s). Data from the 14 settings were collected using a framework to ensure comparable data which would allow for across-case study comparisons. Using these data, centres were then compared in terms of the following eight key characteristics:

- centre profile
- staffing
- 'play'room organization
- parental involvement
- ethos
- curriculum
- pedagogy
- community outreach or involvement.

The literature on school effectiveness and improvement points to the crucial importance of these domains in promoting positive child outcomes and quality experiences for children. Most of this literature has been based on research evidence from primary and secondary school studies; the EPPE and REPEY studies were the first research projects to use this kind of framework in early years research. The importance of using this framework is that the research observations were based on existing information on what research has shown is important in terms of effectiveness and quality.

The REPEY study takes both the quantitative data (child outcomes) and qualitative data collected in conjunction with the EPPE study, and performs a secondary analysis with the objective of exploring issues of leadership within these early years settings. The REPEY research aimed to identify, from a *bottom-up* approach, exemplars of practice and processes which appear to be associated with the moderate to effective quality of the setting. The data used to fulfil this aim were not collected in an effort to directly assess the leadership or its influence upon quality, within the case study settings.

While semi-structured interviews were conducted with the leaders from each of the case study settings, the questions were not explicitly about leadership; rather, they prompted these managers to discuss general quality and effectiveness around topics such as the influence of the Curriculum Guidance for the Foundation Stage (CGFS), staff–child ratios, staff training and development, child development, pedagogy and policy development. The added analysis of interviews with practitioners/staff and parents allowed for a cross-setting analysis, where any contradictions or concurrence between theory and practice or between staff, parent and manager views within a setting could be revealed. In addition to the analyses of interview data, case study information from staff and child observations, documents such as policies, field notes and Ofsted reports were also re-analysed. The framework followed in the REPEY study, described above, was beneficial in that it offered comparative information across each of the settings involved in the study in these key domains, for example, pedagogy and parental involvement. In addition to comparability, the framework offered what Geertz (1973) refers to as 'thick description'. The data-set provided rich and thick description from several sources which offered an insight into the practices and processes of the leaders in the settings.

The aim of the interrogation was to identify within the data what effective leadership practice looks like in early years settings. Rather than taking a completely 'grounded' approach, i.e., one which is explicitly emergent, the researchers began with an 'orienting theory'. During the process of interrogating the data the 'orienting theory' would be constantly adjusted as new categories and/or relationships emerged from the data.

Consultation of the literature was an essential phase in developing an 'orienting theory'. The review included a trawl of the library for landmark studies and relevant books and research journals about leadership. Searches were also conducted via the internet and government websites and publications. In response to the paucity of evidence-based literature relating to early years settings in the area of leadership and management, the researchers consulted leadership and management literature in both primary and secondary schools, with due caution and relevance to the early years context.

The literature on effective leadership points to several key characteristics associated with effective and less effective leadership (Leithwood and Riehl, 2003; Rodd, 1998, 2013). The characteristics are comprehensive but not exhaustive; indeed some caution is advised against the pursuit of an exhaustive list, which could lead to the disregard of contextual circumstances in place of satisfying a 'recipe' for success (Southworth, 2004). Three main functions of leadership and management seem to emerge from the literature. These are, *providing direction, exercising influence* and *improving outcomes*. After considering these characteristics of effective leadership practice, the researchers decided to categorize them under each of these main headings to reflect key concepts within effective leadership (adapted from Leithwood and Riehl, 2003):

- providing setting direction
- exercising influence and developing people
- developing the organization.

Providing setting direction

A key area of leadership practice is the process of identifying and co-creating a shared set of objectives for an early years setting, for children and staff, and inspiring others with a vision of a better future by:

- identifying and articulating a collective vision
- promoting passion for early childhood care and education
- ensuring shared understandings, meanings and goals
- effective communication through transparent systems, openness, honesty and accessibility
- being contextually literate through evidence-based practice and vision
- being reflective, empathic, thoughtful, contemplative and considerate.

Exercising influence and developing people

The success of a setting is dependent upon the level of commitment and effort made by the people within it. This commitment and effort will be endorsed and promoted by the effective positional leader who recognizes the current, as well as potential, strengths of the human resources within a setting by:

- a commitment to ongoing, professional development

- a commitment and focus upon teaching and learning for all

- monitoring and assessing practice

- acting as an exemplar and role model

- influencing others in a moral and purposeful way.

Developing the organization

Leaders of early years settings need to be devoted and committed to promoting and developing the early years setting as a community, rather than an organization, regarding the setting as an organized body that is continually evolving and changing. The leader and or leaders need to encourage and promote the building of relationships among all key players, both within and outside the setting, with practitioners, parents and other stakeholders, such as other agencies and multi-professionals, school governors and management committees, by:

- building a learning community and team culture through collaborative processes

- encouraging and facilitating parent and community partnerships

- planning and managing change in flexible and adjustable ways

- promoting a caring ethos and environment, meeting the needs of all groups

- demonstrating effective leadership and management skills.

Within each of these key concepts, sub-concepts emerged which allowed for further reduction of the data which would subsequently allow for additional searches to be made to explore the data.

The REPEY study was informed by existing research, and literature in school leadership is concerned with its focus and fascination with leaders, particularly head teachers (Southworth, 2004). Southworth goes on to highlight the flaws of this focus in so much that the emphasis placed on the leader allows for the perpetuation of the trait theory of leadership; leaders are born not made. This view of leaders in conjunction with the tendency of research to focus upon the leader rather than the *context* within which she works, including the setting's size, staff, children, families, other stakeholders, location and resources, seems to support the pursuit of identifying key traits of the 'effective leader' which can then be applied, like a recipe, to others in leadership positions. The danger of this is, of course, as highlighted by Southworth (2004), the failure to consider the importance of *context* and its influence as well as its needs when determining leadership requirements. There is a generally accepted view that 'where there are good schools there are good leaders' (Spillane et al., 2004: 14) and there is emerging evidence that illustrates the 'how' of school leadership, that is, knowledge of the ways in which school leaders develop and sustain those conditions and processes believed necessary for innovation and change.

The Effective Leadership in the Early Years Sector (ELEYS study)

The ELEYS study (Siraj-Blatchford and Manni, 2007: 2–3) builds upon the REPEY study, focusing upon *leadership for learning*. The qualitative methodology used in the research study drew upon a sample of settings that had been identified as 'effective' in the EPPE study. A distinctive feature of data analysis in the ELEYS study explored the issue of leadership within *effective* early years settings from the *bottom up*. This approach focused upon concrete leadership behaviours rather than eliciting leadership beliefs. Semi-structured interviews had been conducted with leaders from each of the REPEY case study settings. The questions were not specifically about leadership, but encouraged the managers to discuss their general practice about curriculum, pedagogy, provision, practice, child development, staff ratios, staff training and development. The re-analysis of interviews with early years staff and parents allowed for analysis across and within the settings, providing a means of triangulation, so that contradictions or concurrence between theory and practice between staff, parent or manager perceptions could be revealed.

To identify the contribution made by effective leadership to the success of the REPEY settings, the ELEYS study drew upon the following:

- demographic information about managers
- semi-structured interviews with managers, teachers and other early years staff, for example, nursery nurses and parents
- researcher observations and field notes
- the early years setting's policies and documentation
- child outcome data associated with cognitive and social/behavioural development
- leadership literature in the early years, primary and secondary phases of education.

A specialist early years focus group of service users, heads of settings and stakeholders within the early years sector provided a forum to clarify, construct meaning and validate research findings. Through discussion it became clear that, to demonstrate practices associated with effective leadership, the data should be immersed in context with contextual information, for example, type of setting and funding of provider. An iterative approach to data analysis using progressive engagements with the data, relevant literature on educational leadership and consultative discussions with the early years focus group provided a means for triangulation and validation of data (Siraj-Blatchford and Manni, 2007: 2–3). Key findings demonstrated requirements and characteristics of caring and effective settings in the leadership for learning (Siraj-Blatchford and Manni, 2007: 12).

Requirements for leadership for learning:

- contextual literacy, understanding the setting's community

- a commitment to collaboration

- a commitment to the improvement of children's learning outcomes.

The ELEYS study identified a range of categories of effective leadership practice.

Categories of effective leadership practice:

- identifying and articulating a collective vision

- ensuring shared understandings, meanings and goals

- effective communication

- encouraging reflection

- monitoring and assessing practice

- commitment to ongoing professional development

- distributed leadership

- building a learning community and team culture

- encouraging parent and community partnerships

- leading and managing: striking the balance.

These requirements and categories for effective leadership practices are discussed further in the Model of Effective and Caring Leadership Practices in Part 2 of this book.

Leadership of Learning in Early Years Practice (LLEaP project)

The requirements and categories for effective leadership practices in the leadership for learning in the ELEYS study became a framework for analysis in the research study, the LLEaP project (Hallet and Roberts-Holmes, 2010).

The study investigated the leadership style and practices of graduate early years leaders, who were EYPs in one local authority in England. All the graduate early years leaders in the research sample, worked in non-maintained settings providing sessional and full daycare, and in children's centres. Participants were able to respond freely by recording their under-standing of EYPs' leadership of practice role through qualitative methodology. A grounded theory approach (Charmaz, 2005) to analysis of data identified emerging themes (Yin, 2003) to illuminate the leadership role of early years leaders with EYPS.

The research study was a qualitative case study undertaken in three phases. The first two phases collected data. During phase 1 the data analysis informed the following collection of data in phase 2. Phase 3 of the study was the development and production of a professional learning resource of six case study settings demonstrating effective early years leaders' style and practices in the leadership of learning.

An overview of the research study

Phase 1:

- One leadership workshop
- Analysis of data and six case studies of best leadership practice identified
- Two reflective leadership workshops
- Reflective diary
- Analysis of data.

Phase 2:

- One questionnaire
- Analysis of data.

Phase 3:

- filming of leadership practices in case study settings
- development of the professional learning resource.

An aim of the research study was to identify 'best leadership practice'. The term 'best practice' is used in the early years sector to denote effective ways found in research and professional practice in delivering services (Reardon,

2009). The methodology and analysis around identifying 'best leadership practice' informed the development of a book and a DVD as professional learning resources for exisiting and aspiring leaders (Hallet, 2014). The themes of change and professional development as a leader formed a focus for reflection within the workshops. From the graduate leaders' reflections through focus group discussions in Phase 1, six case studies of best *leadership of learning* practices in early years settings were identified, using the 'requirements for leadership for learning' and categories for 'effective leadership practices' in the ELEYS study as a framework for identifying 'best leadership practice.'

The six graduate women leaders demonstrating 'best leadership practice' in the LLEaP project were representative of the predominantly female early years workforce (Nutbrown, 2011). They worked in a pre-school, a nursery classroom, two community-based playgroups and two day nurseries, in rural and urban contexts. These early years leaders demonstrated they were *leading learning* in their settings and children's centres, for children, parents and carers and practitioners. Their effective leadership practices emerged in eight areas of expertise:

- leading pedagogy in settings

- leading pedagogy for transition

- leading children's learning in the outdoor environment

- leading a learning culture and community of practice

- leading continuing professional learning

- leading, creating and sharing knowledge with parents

- leading change for transformation

- leading creating and sharing reflections.

These leadership of learning practices are discussed further within in the subsequent chapters in Part 2 of this book.

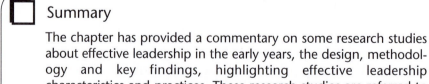

Summary

The chapter has provided a commentary on some research studies about effective leadership in the early years, the design, methodology and key findings, highlighting effective leadership characteristics and practices. These research studies are referred to in subsequent chapters; therefore, the discussion in this chapter forms a backdrop of contextual information for Part 2.

The next section is an introduction to Part 2 of the book, 'Effective early childhood leadership'. The introduction provides an overview of four leadership themes and eight leadership practices in the Model of Effective and Caring Leadership Practices in Early Childhood which forms the content of Part 2.

Further reading

Hallet, E. (2014) *Leadership of Learning in Early Years Practice*. London: Institute of Education Press.
   This book and DVD of examples of leadership practice report the research study of the LLEaP project. They can be used as resources for professional reflection, learning and development.
Moyles, J. (2006) *Effective Leadership and Management in the Early Years*. Maidenhead: Open University Press.
   This book conceptualizes effective leadership and management as a tree with the four key 'branches' of effective leadership and management, defined as leadership qualities, management skills, professional attributes and personal characteristics and attributes.
Siraj-Blatchford, I. and Manni, L. (2007) *Effective Leadership in the Early Years Sector (The ELEYS study)*. London: Institute of Education: University of London.
   This book is the research report of the ELEYS study.
Sylva, K., Melhuish, E., Sammons, P., Siraj-Blatchford, I. and Taggart, B. (2010) *Early Childhood Matters*. Abingdon: Routledge.
   This book provides a comprehensive overview of the EPPE study.

Part 2

Effective early childhood leadership

Introduction

A Model of Effective and Caring Leadership Practices in Early Childhood constitutes Part 2 of the book. The four leadership themes and eight leadership practices shown in Figure 2.1 provide a framework for early childhood leaders to understand further the phenomena of early years leadership.

Leadership themes	Leadership practices
Directional leadership	▪ Developing a shared vision ▪ Effective communication
Collaborative leadership	▪ Promoting a team culture ▪ Promoting parental collaboration
Empowering leadership	▪ Promoting agency ▪ The process of change
Pedagogical leadership	▪ Leading learning ▪ Reflective learning

Figure 2.1 Model of Effective and Caring Leadership Practices in Early Childhood

The following eight chapters provide a practice-based understanding of effective and caring leadership practices for improving quality provision, educational, healthy and well-being outcomes for children. Case studies provide examples of early years leaders leading practice, and reflective questions provide opportunity for existing and aspiring leaders to reflect upon the leadership themes and practices.

The next chapter defines the leadership theme *directional leadership* in effective and caring leadership practices in the early years, examining the leadership practice of *developing a shared vision* within staff and stakeholders within an early years setting, children's centre or school.

3

Directional leadership: developing a shared vision

Chapter overview

The theme of *directional leadership* in effective and caring leadership is defined and the leadership practice of *developing a shared vision* explored. The ability for a leader to develop and articulate a shared vision is central in directional leadership, providing a purposeful pathway for policy, provision and practice within the early years setting, children's centre or school. The importance and process of developing a shared, collective vision by ensuring shared meanings and goals with staff, parents, carers and stakeholders are discussed in this chapter.

This chapter will:

- discuss the development and articulation of vision within directional leadership
- consider an example of directional leadership practice
- provide opportunity to reflect upon directional leadership and developing a shared vision.

Vision within directional leadership

Vision is a critical feature of effective leadership found in successful organizations; this vision needs to be clearly articulated and should be connected to the needs of the setting, school or children's centre, learning and teaching, pedagogy, provision and practice. In the REPEY research case studies, a key area of leadership practice in the early years involved the identification and co-construction by children, staff, parents and carers of shared objectives that provide direction in leadership. Effective leaders inspire others with a vision or a view of a better future, providing focus and motivation for development and growth within a setting, children's centre or school. This relies on a level of dedication and passion about early childhood care and education, and the capacity to reflect upon research and professional practice. The provision of a clear pathway of direction for a setting, children's centre or school is promoted by the leader's capacity to articulate a collective vision that is owned by all staff, children, stakeholders, parents and carers, to ensure consistency among the staff of shared understanding of setting practices, policy and processes, and by being a reflective practitioner and encouraging reflective practice in others (Siraj-Blatchford and Manni, 2007). The vision needs to be clearly articulated, convincing and compelling, and, most importantly, connected to the issues of teaching and learning.

The following case study from the LLEaP project is an early years leader's reflection about her directional leadership, in which she considers her role in developing a shared vision with her nursery team.

 ## Case study: Leader's reflection – directional leadership

Amana is an early years leader in a private daycare nursery; she reflects upon her leadership style, the influences upon her own vision for children's learning and development, and how she influences others in developing a shared vision within her nursery staff team. She illustrates her directional leadership style and vision for her nursery pictorially using the image of a plant (Figure 3.1), to depict the growth of children's learning and development and the nursery setting as a developing, growing organization.

Before I begin a reflection about me as a leader, I feel compelled to point out that there is no 'I' in our team, so although this reflection is related to my leadership, this leadership style has been developed to suit the context and needs of the people in our setting. This style needs to be flexible in relation to the setting and also the staff, families and children who grow and change within it.

I feel I have a sound level of confidence and knowledge and understanding of the early years in my own vision in terms of ideology, personal views and values. A good leader has to match this personal stance to the setting and I feel passion towards sharing my vision with all involved in the setting.

I feel I plant the seeds and try to become the underlying (and often invisible) roots that underpin and hold together the growing and developing plant, which is the nursery. Although these roots, such as commitment, vision, innovation, belief, knowledge and understanding, are often invisible, my leadership style is very visible in terms of a fundamental belief that I must lead by example, as an excellent role model and demonstrate my *vision for best practice* for all involved in our setting.

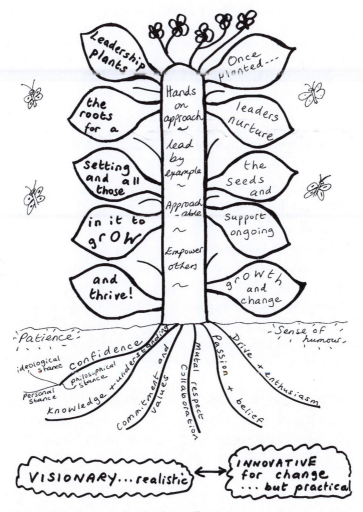

Figure 3.1 Amana's leadership reflection

To be able to do this, there are many personal qualities I feel I need to be able to use. Firstly, drive and enthusiasm, if I don't show enthusiasm towards change and leading learning, I can't expect the team to do so. I'm happy to lead by example, to develop the team's confidence and also their knowledge and understanding which then impacts positively upon their values, beliefs and practice. However, I

(Continues)

(Continued)

am also aware of my limitations. I am visionary, but sometimes need my team (particularly Karen) to make me develop my sense of realism!

My final reflection about leadership relates to my drawing. Leadership plants the roots that hold the setting in place but it is the whole team, staff, children and families that allow a setting to grow, change and thrive! Everyone makes the plant survive and grow by watering it with their knowledge, understanding and expertise of working with young children and families. The butterflies represent the flitting nature of leadership, having to be part of so much and have so many different roles but that is also what makes it so very exciting.

The following questions will enable reflection for existing and aspiring leaders to consider their vision for working with children and families.

 Questions for reflection

For existing leaders

- What are the influences upon your vision?
- How do you articulate this vision and ensure this becomes a collective vision, shared understandings and meanings?
- How is your vision integrated within your leadership style and practice?

For aspiring leaders

Reflect upon your own vision for your work with children and families.

- What are the influences upon your vision?
- How is your vision integrated within your provision and practice?
- Do you articulate or demonstrate your vision to others, if so how?

Developing a shared vision

In order to ensure the achievement of set targets and desired outcomes, a clear vision must exist. Without it, those within an organization will often be working towards different and at times conflicting agendas. They will be led by their own vision of what early years practice should look like, rather than by a vision that has been devised through consultation with current research, key players, stakeholders and consideration of the context. But how can a clear vision emerge?

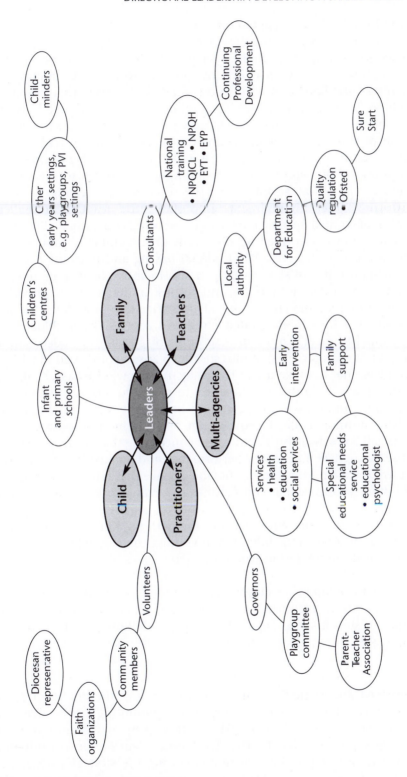

Figure 3.2 Early years stakeholders

In the DfES (2005b) draft paper entitled 'Championing children: a shared set of skills, knowledge and behaviours for managers of integrated children's service', one key aspect of leadership highlighted is the provision of direction. *Providing direction* is one of the two overarching functions of leadership as highlighted by Leithwood and Riehl (2003) in their summary of findings from several leadership studies. It is argued that it is the responsibility of the leader(s) to help determine and articulate the vision, as well as play an active role in making the vision a reality. It is also noted that it is crucial that the leader(s) possess an understanding of the needs and aspirations of children and their families in order to ensure the capacity to think strategically about the services their setting provides. Southworth (2004) highlights as important, the leader's or leaders' possession of context-specific knowledge and being contextually literate so that their vision is informed by the needs of the children, families and community which it serves. The leader(s) having and pursuing a vision, should demonstrate collaborative, open and inclusive behaviour, towards building a common understanding and purpose in the pursuit of providing clear and purposeful direction. A list of aims related to providing clear and purposeful direction in integrated children's centres (DfES, 2005b) has been adapted to meet a more diverse range of providers. Leaders should aim to translate strategic vision into specific plans in collaboration with all stakeholders, that is, make use of the collective knowledge base, challenge the status quo and do things differently to meet the specific needs of the children and families within the setting more effectively. Build a shared value base; promote collective knowledge and common purpose. Support others to talk knowledgably about issues concerning their work and area of expertise. Recognize that service performance and quality of provision can be improved via a responsive and flexible service that reflects the needs of the children, young people and families it serves. Work for equality and inclusiveness of service. Develop a culture of, and systems to support a high level of, responsiveness within the setting. Know the legislative frameworks for services to children and young people, and know where to go for detailed interpretation when required.

These aims focus upon developing an informed vision. Arguably, in the early years sector this requires a more overt and concerted consideration of the input of stakeholders. Figure 3.2 on page 41 illustrates the extensive array of stakeholders, leaders and staff in the early years sector.

An informed and shared vision assists in focusing the attention of all relevant stakeholders on what is important, promoting a reflective staff who are motivated to reach goals and objectives, leading towards translating vision into reality, that have been identified in consultation with all who are responsible for implementing the strategies needed to reach the desired goals. While there is general acceptance of the importance of vision, without the process of consultation, observation and reflection, the resulting vision, no matter to what degree the vision links to literature and research, will be an inadequate and uninformed vision.

Consultation towards a shared vision

Consulting with staff, parents and stakeholders is an essential method of ensuring improvement and effectiveness, and for promoting shared understandings and identifying common objectives with staff. Research on school improvement and effectiveness suggests that where staff have been involved in the development of guidelines and policy for their school, setting or children's centre, there was likely to be an organization-wide consistency in guideline usage and implementation of policy into practice, whereas when staff had not been involved, there was likely to be variation, with teachers and practitioners tending to adopt individual approaches to the use of guidelines and policies for different curriculum areas. It appears, therefore, that staff involvement was related to a more consistent school-setting- and centre-based approach to the curriculum. It is critically important in building teams that individual members of a team share a common understanding of the organization, its aims and ways of working (Bennett et al., 2003). Figure 3.3 illustrates the process of promoting a shared and collective vision. The agency of stakeholders is important to dissipate dissension, to reflect upon the vision and integrate it into provision and practice, so the outcome is the whole staff team working together in agreed action, moving together in concertive action.

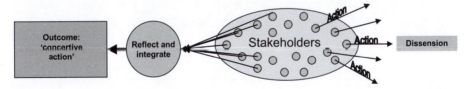

Figure 3.3 Promoting a shared collective vision

Vision into policy and practice

Strategies, development plans, improvement plans and policies are processes and procedures for leaders to provide directional leadership in a planned and purposeful way to meet aims and objectives defined within the collective shared vision. A policy is a document which provides a cohesive framework for the delivery of curriculum, cross-curricular themes such as safeguarding children, equality, health and well-being. Similarly, the school, setting or children's centre development or improvement plan provides a framework for implementing the collective vision into a planned integration into provision and practice. This plan should be a working document with long-, medium-

and short-term planning, a strategic action plan for improving policy and practice underpinned by the shared vision.

The following reflective questions will help you to reflect upon your school, setting or children's centre strategies and leadership for implementing shared vision into provision and practice. What process do they provide for directional leadership?

 Questions for reflection

For existing and aspiring leaders

Reflect upon your school, setting or children's centre strategies for making shared vision into reality.

- What strategies are in place?
- How were you consulted in the development of them?
- Do you feel involved in implementing the strategies? If so, how?
- Consider your setting, school or children's centre development or improvement plan. How does this provide a directional framework for implementing vision into provision and practice?
- Who provides directional leadership in the development or improvement plan? Is this shared, distributed leadership or not?
- How effective is the directional leadership in providing a purposeful direction for your setting, school or children's centre?
- Consider if an Ofsted inspector walked into your setting, school or children's centre would they know about your organization's vision? How would this be articulated to them?

Summary

Directional leadership and developing shared vision have been the focus of the discussion in this chapter. The process of developing a shared collective vision through consultation with staff and stakeholders, articulating and implementing vision through strategies, and making the vision into reality within provision and practice has been explored. A case study of an early years leader's directional leadership and reflective questions has provided the opportunity for reflective consideration about the process of developing a shared vision in directional leadership.

→ The next chapter continues the discussion about *directional leadership*, focusing upon the importance of *effective communication* in developing and articulating a collective vision with shared meaning and understanding.

Further reading

Ang, L. (2010) 'Critical perspectives on cultural diversity in early childhood: building an inclusive curriculum and provision', *Early Years*, 30(1): 41–52.

This journal article explores the challenges of developing an effective early years provision and pedagogy that values cultural difference within the framework of a mandated curriculum.

Beckley, P. (2012) 'Historical Perspectives', in P. Beckley (ed.), *Learning in Early Childhood*. London: Sage. pp. 5–17.

This chapter considers historical, contemporary and international perspectives relevant to challenges faced by leaders and practitioners and how they impact upon care and education for young children.

Canning, N. (2012) 'Exploring the concept of quality play', in M. Reed and N. Canning (eds), *Implementing Quality Improvement and Change in the Early Years*. London: Sage. pp. 75–91.

This chapter provides an overview of principles of play provision in the early years to support the development of a direction and vision.

Priest, K., King, S., Nangala, I., Nungurrayi Brown, W. and Nangala, M. (2008) 'Warrki Jarrinjaku "working together everyone listening": growing together as leaders for Aboriginal children in remote central Australia', *European Early Childhood Education Research Journal*, 16(1): 117–130.

This journal article outlines an early childhood leadership model that senior Anangu and Yapa (Aboriginal) women living semi-traditional lifestyles in the remote desert regions of central Australia have identified as a positive and important way forward for their children.

Directional leadership: effective communication

Chapter overview

The leadership practice of *effective communication* within the *directional leadership* theme in effective and caring leadership in the early years is discussed in this chapter. Leaders' ability to communicate effectively is clearly linked to the articulation of vision to all stakeholders, including children, influencing others and promoting consistency in policy, provision and practice. This chapter explores ways of communicating effectively and the role of emotional intelligence in directional leadership.

This chapter will:

* explore effective communication in directional leadership

* consider the role of active listening in effective communication

* examine emotional intelligence within leadership

* provide an opportunity to reflect upon effective communication in directional leadership.

Communicating and connecting with others

'Effective communication forms a fundamental part of the early years practitioner's role' and, arguably, drives practitioners' and leaders' roles in working with children and families within a people-centred service (Rose and Rogers, 2012: 51). Rose and Rogers (2012) identify seven dimensions of the practitioner's role working in early years settings: the critical reflector, the carer, *the communicator*, the facilitator, the observer, the assessor and the creator. As a communicator, the practitioner communicates with children, parents and carers, agencies, staff and others in verbal and non-verbal ways. Their two-way communication process enables them to connect with others through reciprocal relationships. The quality of interactions is crucial for effective communication to take place. Practitioners and leaders should be aware of their interactions and reflect upon the effectiveness of these interactions for children's educational, health, social and well-being.

The central importance of communication in the range of practitioners' roles in children and young people's services is promoted in the *Common Core of Skills and Knowledge for the Children's Workforce* (CCSK) (DfES, 2005c). The CCSK emerged from the *Every Child Matters* strategy (DfES, 2004b) providing a common set of knowledge and skills for those working with children and young people from birth to 19 years of age in England. The six themes within the CCSK reflect a set of common values for practitioners that promote equality, reflect diversity and challenge stereotypes, helping to improve the life chances of all children and young people and to provide more effective integrated services. The first theme, 'Effective communication and engagement with children, young people their families and carers' states that:

> Good communication is central to working with children and young people, involving listening, questioning, understanding and responding to what is being communicated by children, young people and those caring for them. It is important to be able to communicate both on a one-on-one basis and in a group context. Communication is not just about the words you use, but also the manner of your speaking, body language and, above all, the effectiveness with which you listen. To communicate effectively it is important to take account of culture and context, for example where English is an additional language. (DfES, 2005c: 6)

These skills and knowledge are developed through training, reflective learning and experience. The skills and knowledge required for working with children and young people include (DfES, 2005c: 7–9):

Skills

- listening and building empathy

- summarizing and explaining

- consultation and negotiation

Knowledge

- how communication works

- confidentiality and ethics

- sources of support

- importance of respect.

Similarly, communication is central to leadership, particularly in articulating shared vision in providing a direction for the setting, school or children's centre. Communication in relationship to a leader's role has the same purpose as in a practitioner's role, that is, to connect with others. Leaders will also communicate within a wider field of early years stakeholders, as shown in Figure 3.2. The way leaders communicate effectively in directional leadership is now discussed.

Effective communication within directional leadership

'Successful leadership in the early childhood field is a matter of communication more than anything else' (Rodd, 2013: 63). Early childhood services are concerned with people, where relationships, communication and interpersonal skills form the structure of services for young children and families. The importance of the leader's or leaders' capability to communicate clearly is essential. A leader who is capable of communicating clearly to all stakeholders, including children, is also likely to command greater capacity to influence and not manipulate others. Communication includes the capacity to listen to and take seriously the concerns and issues raised by all stakeholders. The capacity to communicate clearly is invariably linked to the articulation of vision and directional leadership. The key to achieving outcomes is the capacity to provide, for all relevant stakeholders, clarity about what must be achieved and the direction of travel.

With the continual influx of government reviews and policies it is essential that leaders act as the intermediary, summarizing and making sense of the policies to all relevant stakeholders in their current context, using clear communication to reduce the feeling of working to different and conflicting agendas among those in a setting, school or children's centre. The leader's role is to provide a forum for open discourse among staff members, and to identify barriers to communication and strategies to overcome these barriers. Leadership as the management of meaning (Fairhurst, 2011) becomes explicit in how leaders use their everyday talk and carry out interactions with others. Leadership as the management of meaning for direction is not solely concerned with leading change, but is grounded in everyday routine and mundane aspects of the leader's role, as the following case study shows.

Case study: Leadership as the management of meaning

Jasintha is a newly appointed head teacher of a nursery school. She is in her first term of headship and is reflecting upon the provision and practice she finds in the nursery school she came to. Her vision and direction of travel for pedagogy, provision and practice in the nursery school are driven by her image and construct of a young child:

> Each child is unique, with a voice and rights to be respected within the context of their culture and family. The nursery school aims to provide a rich environment to enable the growth of every child through equal access and opportunity to a broad curriculum.

This image provided the framework for her child-centred approach to teaching and learning in a nursery school in which children are at the centre of all that happens within the nursery school. Pedagogy reflected in the Early Years Foundation Stage curriculum (DCSF, 2008b) promoted child-led activity, placing the child at the centre of the curriculum, and this is reflected in Jasintha's vision. An individually held vision by a head teacher was insufficient for her directional leadership; she needed to effectively communicate this vision, so it became an understood and shared collective vision within her nursery. She typed out her vision statement onto laminated cards to use with the staff team in discussion groups at the next staff meeting. Through the discussion, she wanted the staff to unpick her vision statement, gain meaning and understanding of her vision, then reconstruct it into a collective vision with meaning shared and understood by all. The final vision statement may or may not be the same, but will be owned by all.

The unique child is at the centre of her vision. In implementing her vision statement into practice, Jasintha wanted the children's many 'voices' to be integral throughout the nursery school, for example, for children's drawings and paintings to be displayed and their writing in books for children to read in the book corner. She was aware that traditionally some nursery nurses in the nursery school were used to proudly displaying their own artwork in friezes illustrating nursery rhymes, rather than spending time mounting and displaying children's drawings and paintings, which would send a message that children's artwork was valued and respected. This practice was the essence of her vision of a child-centred provision for young children which gave direction to her leadership. How could she lead and manage the staff's meaning and understanding of this vision, providing directional leadership, implementing vision into pedagogy and practice, without offending any one?

(Continues)

(Continued)

Jasintha developed a strategy to sensitively articulate and communicate her vision into practice. She regularly worked with children in activities alongside practitioners. At these times she discussed planning with the practitioners, and so was beginning to discuss ways of providing child-led activity. While in the learning areas, she began to comment upon the physical environment practitioners had provided. Looking around she enthusiastically praised the children's drawings, paintings, writing and models she could see, purposely omitting to comment upon any of the adults' artwork displayed. Through communicating acknowledgement and verification of valuing, displaying and using children's work as a learning resource, over time Jasintha highlighted practice that gave meaning to her vision and direction in her leadership of the nursery school.

The following questions provide opportunity to reflect upon a way you have led and managed meaning to give direction in pedagogy, provision and practice.

 Questions for reflection

For existing leaders

Reflect upon a way you have led and managed meaning to give direction in pedagogy, provision and practice.

• What strategy did you use to give direction?

• How did you use communication in leading and managing meaning?

• How do you know your directional leadership was effective?

For aspiring leaders

Reflect upon how a leader has provided direction and meaning for you to understand an aspect of pedagogy, provision and practice.

• What communication skills did they use?

• How did they enable you to develop understanding and meaning?

• How effective were the leader's communication skills?

The importance of listening in an active way in effective communication for leaders is now discussed.

Active listening for understanding

Effective communication is multifunctional and multi-directional. It involves the following features: talking, encouraging, questioning, listening, reflecting, translating, interpreting, consulting, debating, summarizing, understanding, acknowledging, negotiating, decision-making, verifying and reporting. Early childhood leaders require knowledge of early childhood, children's learning and development, curriculum, multi-agency working, government policy and specific knowledge of the context in which the communication will take place. In the ELEYS study, evidence of leaders using the features and related outcomes of effective communication was found when leaders provided a level of *transparency* in regard to expectations, practices and processes; there was *reciprocity* in dialogue, and *consultation* and *reflection* with the communication process (Siraj-Blatchford and Manni, 2007). The multi-faceted nature of effective communication is illustrated in Figure 4.1.

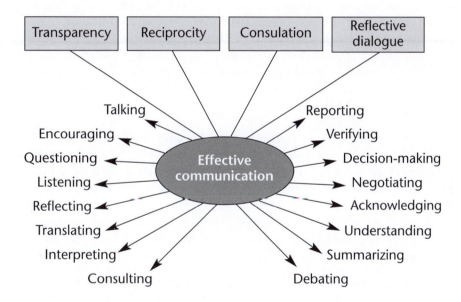

Figure 4.1 Effective communication

The ability to listen effectively, as a leadership attribute, is key to a leader's directional leadership. Effective listening is to actively listen, which is more than hearing words but engaging with the words spoken, gaining meaning and understanding behind the words articulated, and using all information given, including underlying feelings, to understand the meaning of the message as it was intended. This kind of listening for understanding is known as 'active listening' or 'reflective listening' and involves the listener having appropriate time and space to devote to the speaker (Rodd, 2013: 73). This means identifying any barriers to communication, such as an inappropriate environment for communication to take place, a corridor where others pass and may overhear, answering the telephone or emails, background noise, an uncommon first language, or visual or hearing difficulties. Barriers to communication can be overcome, for example, by having a specific time when uninterrupted meetings can be held. The listener receives non-verbal and verbal messages from the speaker as well as listening to the content of the message, and will respond in appropriate ways. The listener uses verbal and non-verbal information to reflect upon and interpret the message, responding to clarify meaning and understanding. The speaker similarly uses verbal and non-verbal cues to respond to the listener's communication.

Communication is a reflective process that takes time to develop through reciprocal relationships. Sustained Shared Thinking emerged from the REPEY project – an episode of interactions in which two or more individuals 'work together' in a cognitive dance to solve a problem, clarify a concept and evaluate activities. It is usual for Sustained Shared Thinking to be associated with interactions between children and adults, or children and children (Rose and Rogers, 2012: 79) as a scaffolding process to develop cognitive thinking. However, Sustained Shared Thinking as effective communication between adults and adults is reciprocal reflective dialogue; adults mutually construct meaning and understanding together (Siraj-Blatchford et al., 2002).

The way the listener responds to the speaker and how the speaker responds to the listener can help or hinder in the co-construction of meaning. Carl Rogers (1961) identifies five response styles commonly used in verbal communication in people-centred organizations (adapted from Rodd, 2013: 74):

- *Advising and evaluating.* The purpose of the response is to give advice – 'What you should do now, if I were you ...'.

- *Interpreting and analysing.* The purpose of the response is to interpret information given – 'The real issue here is ...'.

- *Supporting and placating.* The purpose of the response is to diminish emotions – 'Don't worry, it'll be OK'.

- *Questioning and probing.* The purpose of the response is to gain more information. 'Is everything all right at home?'

- *Understanding or reflecting.* The purpose of the response is to focus on the underlying feelings as well as the content. 'You seem to be pleased about how Ben is progressing with his reading ...'.

The appropriateness of response type is the hallmark of a highly sophisticated and competent professional communicator (Rodd, 2013). An effective leader gives directional leadership through advice, evaluation, support, questioning, understanding and reflection. Working in a people-centred service provides early years leaders with work-related pressures and stresses which can be emotionally taxing and affect communication. The role of emotion in leadership is now discussed.

Emotional intelligence within leadership

There is a unique emotional drive in the early years, often described as *passion* in working with young children and families. The term is often used by early years practitioners and leaders to describe their agency of working in the early years sector. Passion was evidenced as a key driver for working and leading in the early years sector in the LLEaP research study (Hallet, 2014). Similarly, Moyles (2006) in identifying leadership attributes in the Effective Leadership and Management Scheme for the Early Years (ELMS-EY) found successful leaders are those who have a 'deep-seated passion' for the children, school and community in which they work (Moyles, 2006: 9).

It is recognized that young children need to be cared for in order to survive, and have positive emotional attachments with significant caring adults (Bowlby, 1988). A supportive, caring and sensitive environment is important for young children's development (Osgood, 2006); caring, physical interactions such as rocking, cuddling and physical games with young children stimulate positive physical and intellectual development (Manning-Morton, 2006). Elfer (2012) argues that working with emotion is integral to working with young children. In the training of nursery nurses and teaching assistants on further education courses, caring attributes such as warmth, emotion, nurturing, sensitivity and care are encouraged in students (Colley, 2006). The use of emotional labour offers opportunities for young women from low socio-economic backgrounds to raise their self-esteem and self-worth within a work context of status such as a school (Vincent and Braun, 2010) and form a self-identity of a caring practitioner.

Emotionality can be regarded as un-intellectual and promotes the idea of emotional labour as intuitive to women's way of working (Taggart, 2011). Early years practitioners and leaders confidently work with emotion in order to provide the best care and education for young children. Working with young children is physical, intellectual and emotional. Practitioners' and leaders' in their daily work deal with emotional situations, for example, a hurt and crying child, an angry parent or a safeguarding issue, requiring emotional skills of the highest calibre (Osgood, 2011). It is each practitioner's and leader's ability to manage their own feelings, and identify and respond sensitively to others' feelings in a professional manner, that is essential in effective communication and in resolving conflict. Goleman (1996) describes this as emotional intelligence and it is demonstrated in effective leaders. Leaders need to be self-aware of their emotional state and manage their feelings accordingly, or insensitivity and an inappropriate response by a leader can be a barrier to effective communication and the message being received appropriately (Rodd, 2013). Reciprocal communication in which a leader has the ability to listen empathetically is a skill effective leaders possess (Goleman, 1996).

Leaders can be appointed for their academic ability, their previous experience or becoming a leader through a vacant situation arising. They will not become successful leaders if they have not developed considerable emotional intelligence for leading within the people-centred service in which they work (Rodd, 2013). Emotional intelligence is the aptitude that affects all other leadership abilities, either enhancing or interfering with them (Goleman, 1996). Emotionally intelligent leaders can raise standards, encourage personal and professional growth, and foster organizational sustainability. Emotionally literate leaders also appreciate the need to support emotional competences within their staff and through them contribute to building an emotionally competent organization (Rodd, 2013). Goleman (1996) describes emotional intelligence as knowing your feelings, being able to manage your emotions, having a sense of empathy, being able to repair emotional damage in yourself and in others, and being emotionally interactive by tuning into people so that you can interact with them effectively.

Effective communication skills underpin emotionally intelligent leaders who are able to talk about their own feelings in an assertive way, are good listeners and responders, ask appropriate questions and engage in a meaningful dialogue. An emotionally intelligent leader nurtures and values the emotional intelligence of staff, children and parents, therefore enhancing the capacity of the setting to work in emotionally intelligent ways (Rodd, 2013).

The following reflective questions enable you to reflect upon your own emotional intelligence as a leader or an aspiring leader.

 Questions for reflection

For existing and aspiring leaders
Reflect upon your emotional intelligence, how emotionally literate are you?

- **How well do you know your feelings?**
Rate yourself: 1 – 10 (10 = highest score, 1 = lowest score)

Give an example of how you acknowledged or understood your feelings.

- **How well can you manage your emotions?**

Rate yourself: 1–10 (10 = highest score, 1 = lowest score)

Give an example of how you managed your feelings in communicating with a colleague. Were you pleased or could there be improvement? If so, how?

- **How good is your sense of empathy?**

Rate yourself: 1–10 (10 = highest score, 1 = lowest score)

Give an example of how you showed empathy in communicating with another. Were you pleased or could there be improvement? If so, how?

- **How able are you to repair emotional damage in yourself and in others?**

Rate yourself: 1–10 (10 = highest score, 1 = lowest score)

Give an example of how you repaired emotional damage in yourself and/or in others. Were you pleased or could there be improvement? If so, how?

- **How emotionally interactive are you?**

Rate yourself: 1–10 (10 = highest score, 1 = lowest score)

Give an example of how you were emotionally interactive, tuning into a person's mood, feelings. How did this interaction enable effective or ineffective communication? Were you pleased or could there be improvement? If so, how?

In a review of literature about qualities of effective leaders in early childhood, Rodd (2013: 58) identified common qualities, skills, knowledge and capabilities associated with leadership, these included emotional intelligence and reciprocal communication. Effective leaders were found to demonstrate capability in eight leadership capabilities as shown in Figure 4.2.

The following reflective activity use three of Rodd's leadership capabilities to enable existing and aspiring leaders to reflect upon their leadership capability.

Emotional intelligence
The ability to identify and respond sensitively to one's own and others' feelings

Critical thinking
The ability to influence others through logical and analytical reasoning

Directional clarity
The ability to set, articulate and motivate people to commit to clear goals

Creative intelligence
The ability to solve problems by integrating and applying knowledge, understanding and skills

People enablement
The ability to empower people by offering support and mentoring

Reciprocal communication
The ability to listen empathetically and to network with others

Change orchestration
The ability to lead change proactively and constructively

Perseverance
The capacity to behave assertively, confidently and professionally

Figure 4.2 Effective leadership capabilities (adapted from Rodd, 2013)

Questions for reflection

For existing and aspiring leaders

Leadership capability: emotional intelligence, the ability to identity and respond sensitively to one's own and others' feelings.

- Reflect upon the leadership capability of being emotionally intelligent. Write a short paragraph summarizing your capacity to lead with emotional intelligence.

Leadership capability: directional clarity, the ability to set, articulate and motivate people to commit to clear goals.

- Reflect upon the leadership capability of directional clarity. Write a short paragraph summarizing your capacity to lead with directional clarity.

Leadership capability: reciprocal communication, the ability to listen empathetically and to network with others.

- Reflect upon the leadership capability of reciprocal communication. Write a short paragraph summarizing your capacity to lead with reciprocal communication.

 Summary

This chapter has explored ways of communicating effectively in directional leadership, by actively listening, being emotionally literate and alleviating barriers to communication. A case study demonstrated an early years leader's knowledge, skills and understanding about effective communication in her directional leadership. Reflective questions give opportunity for existing and aspiring leaders to reflect upon their communication knowledge, skills and understanding, and emotional intelligence in their capability of effective communication in directional leadership.

 The next chapter defines the leadership theme, *collaborative leadership* in effective and caring leadership practices, examining the leadership practice of *promoting a team culture* within an early years setting, children's centre or school.

Further reading 📖

Jarvis, J. and Lamb, S. (2001) 'Interaction and the development of communication in the under twos: issues for practitioners working with young children in groups', *Early Years*, 21(2): 129–38.

This journal article considers the role of adult–child interaction in the communication development of children under 2, specifically investigating a family of twins and the ability of adults to undertake sustained, supportive interactions with two children at the same time.

Perry, L., Lennie, C. and Humphrey, N. (2008) 'Emotional literacy in the primary school classroom: teacher perceptions and practices', *Education 3–13*, 36(1): 27–37.

This journal article disseminates research about teachers' perceptions of emotional literacy and how this is modelled in the classroom; findings are discussed in the context of developing emotional literacy in schools.

Rodd, J. (2013) *Leadership in Early Childhood*. 4th edn. Maidenhead: Open University Press. pp. 64–103.

These two chapters in this book discuss early childhood leaders' communication skills: Chapter 4 'Leading through communication: meeting others' needs'; Chapter 5 'Leading through communication: meeting personal needs'.

Rose, J. and Rogers, S. (2012) *The Role of the Adult in Early Years Settings*. Maidenhead: Open University Press. pp. 50–67.

This book presents 'seven selves of the plural practitioner' examining the differing aspects of a practitioner's role in working with children, families and others. Chapter 4 focuses upon 'The communicator' and discusses effective communication.

5

Collaborative leadership: promoting a team culture

Chapter overview

The theme *collaborative leadership* in effective and caring leadership is defined and the leadership practice of *promoting a team culture* explored. The chapter highlights the importance of the promotion of a team culture, with an understanding that successful settings, schools and children's centres rely upon the forging and sustaining of relationships within and beyond the organization. A range of examples of early years leaders' practice demonstrates collaborative leadership, ways to build relationships and promote a team culture. There is opportunity for reflection about leading in a collaborative way, experiencing a team culture and working in a team.

This chapter will:

- define collaborative leadership
- consider ways of building relationships and promoting a team culture
- reflect upon leaders' experiences of collaborative leadership
- provide opportunity for reflection about building relationships and promoting a team culture.

A team culture of collaborative relationships

Working in early childhood services is about working with people: owing to the nature of the work, no one works in isolation but within a network of relationships: parents, staff, children, multi-agencies, governors, management committees, Parent–Teacher Associations (PTAs) and community members. Working within an early years setting, school or children's centre involves many interactions. The quality of relationships and those interactions forms the basis of the quality of the services for young children and families (Rodd, 2013). Early childhood services involve people, relationships and feelings (Jones and Pound, 2008). Central to working in the early years is the collaborative way leaders and practitioners work together through working as a team, and this involves sharing expertise, understanding and reflective dialogue. Leadership in the early childhood field is about the result of groups of people working together through a relational culture of collaboration and teamwork (Rodd, 2013).

Leaders are responsible for a team but can also work within a team as a team member. 'Responsibilities of leaders include a responsibility *to* the team, and a responsibility *for* the team' (emphasis in original) (Jones and Pound, 2008: 25). Bennett et al. (2003: 9) found 'teams operate best in an open climate, with both intra-group and inter-group relations based on mutual trust and open communication in a supportive organizational climate' within a culture of collaboration and leadership that recognizes the strengths and expertise among staff. The effectiveness of the team can depend upon the personal qualities, nature and interventions of the leader to promote a team culture in which all are valued and respected within a climate of trust (Jones and Pound, 2008). Effective leadership enables a team to work collaboratively together in a focused way, sharing their knowledge, skills and understanding for the benefit of the setting, school or children's centre, the families and young children it serves (Harpley and Roberts, 2006). Two early years leaders in the LLEaP project reflect upon their collaborative leadership style and teamwork.

 ## Case study: Leader's reflection – collaborative leadership

Ava is an early years leader in a private day nursery. She has shared leadership with another leader in the leadership team. She works three days in the private day nursery and two days at the local university as a lecturer, teaching on an undergraduate degree course, the BA (Hons) in Early Years.

> My leadership style is quite 'people' orientated. I like to promote a collaborative approach and this enables practice to develop and the team to take ownership of this. I do sometimes find this challenging as naturally my personality is controlling and perfectionist, and I know these traits do not fit in with how I believe I should be a leader!

To promote a collaborative approach, mutual respect between staff, children and families is critical. I need to be (and hopefully am) empathetic to the needs and ideas of my team and ensure I am approachable. I like to think I am happy to take on board and honestly value the ideas of others – willing to try new things as long as we reflect on them afterwards and as a team develop practice accordingly.

I also feel staff need to know I have weaknesses too, as this supports their own confidence and self-esteem. We can giggle about my slightly obsessive behaviour in relation to matching drawing pins ... and this makes me appear human rather than somebody who also lectures at uni and must therefore be on another level. I hate levels – we are all an essential part of a team. However, I also know when the crunch comes, I will lead learning and change. I can handle challenges and confrontation if I need to ... although I'm lucky and very rarely face this.

 ## Case study: Leader's reflection – teamwork

Karen is an early years leader in a voluntary community-based playgroup situated in a village hall. She takes a broad community-based view of team work and reflects upon the centrality of relationships when working in a team.

Teamwork is central to my work as a leader. As a leader I ensure others are valued – staff thoughts, children's thoughts, parents' thoughts, visitors and other professionals. Everyone is valued and involved – their thoughts, their ideas, and their strengths. I try and combine these attributes to bring out the best combination. To do this I develop good relationships with people. I talk to them, I listen, and I am interested in them. I support them, and this can be a two-way process, they support me in the mission and the work of the playgroup. These are some examples of ways I listen and involve parents and carers, children, staff and the playgroup committee so they all feel part of the playgroup team and can contribute to the playgroup.

Parents and carers are listened to and valued

We regard parents and carers as knowing their child best. The playgroup parents are part of the playgroup team, there is a rota for parent duty and parents sign up to help at the playgroup sessions. We have an open-door policy, parents and carers are welcomed into the playgroup to work with the children and to discuss any concerns about their child's progress with us. At arrival and collection time,

(Continues)

(Continued)

the practitioners informally chat with the parents and carers about the activities their child has done that day; any concerns we or the parents and carers have are discussed. We hold an open session at the weekend, for extended family members to come and see the playgroup and the work the children have done. Our aim is to get to know the children's parents, carers and extended family and build positive relationships over time, this supports their child in their play, learning and development.

Children are listened to and valued

We are child centred at the playgroup and our aim is to get to know each child individually and develop positive relationships to facilitate their play, learning and development within the indoor play environment and in the outdoor learning environment. We listen to, respect and value what the children say. The process of their learning and development is showed through photographs shared with parents and carers and in books and posters of their work.

Staff are listened to and valued

Staff use reflection and reflective practice, a climate of trust, reflective conversations, constructive feedback and evaluation to be listened to and valued as a team member. As a leader, I role-model positive interactions, provide opportunity for self-evaluation and reflection daily. The regular staff meetings are led by me or one of the play leaders to develop knowledge and practice.

Playgroup committee are listened to and valued

The playgroup is a voluntary organization based within the community. The playgroup management committee is integral in our playgroup team. A range of parents and volunteers from the community meet regularly to discuss playgroup matters, these may be funding, provision, policy and practice. The committee gives differing perspectives to our work. Members of the playgroup committee are welcomed into the playgroup to see our daily work and to play and work with the children in their learning and development.

The following questions will help you reflect upon your experiences of collaborative leadership and team work.

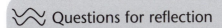

Questions for reflection

For existing and aspiring leaders

You may reflect upon a positive or negative experience or both to compare collaborative leadership practices.

Consider a *positive* experience of collaborative leadership when you felt included in a team and contributed to a team decision or team task.

- Describe your experience in a short piece of narrative writing.
- What did the leader or leaders do to enable you to be part of the team?
- What did the team members do to enable you to be part of the team and contribute to a team decision or team task?
- How did this experience make you feel?

Consider a *negative* experience of collaborative leadership when you felt excluded in a team and contributed little to a team decision or team task.

- Describe your experience in a short piece of narrative writing.
- What did the team members not do to enable you to be part of the team and contribute to a team decision or team task?
- What did the team members not do to enable you to be part of the team and contribute to a team decision or team task?
- How did this experience make you feel?

Working collaboratively in different teams is now discussed.

Leading and working in teams

An early years practitioner can work in a number of teams ranging in size, for example, a small team in a room in a day nursery, a larger team in a Foundation Stage unit in a primary school, a multi-agency team in a children's centre. Even a childminder working in a home setting, seemingly alone, is part of a team inside and outside her home, working with the parents as service users, the local childminder network and her childminder development worker. Whatever context the practitioner works in, she or he is part of an immediate team, a local team and wider teams, within and across early years settings, schools and services. In a revision of the National Standards for Leadership of SureStart Children's Centre Services, the role of leaders leading within, across and beyond children's centres is included in the 'Draft National Standards', developing a network of relationships in children's centre services for systematic and sustainable leadership (Siraj-Blatchford and Hallet, 2012). The professional qualities and skills in these 'Draft National Standards', required for leaders working in children's centre services, include being able to foster and establish an open, inclusive and safe culture of trust, support and respect, promote a collegial approach to decisions but have the confidence to be decisive when necessary, collaborate and negotiate within and beyond the children's centre service, and be able to mediate and manage conflict.

The development of effective relationships between a range of leaders, practitioners, multi-agency professionals, parents and other professionals plays a key role in promoting more consistency in the classroom, early years setting and children's centre. The *Children's and Young People's Workforce Strategy* (DCSF, 2008a) recommends practitioners working with children and young people from birth to 19 years of age to be committed to integrated working with other professionals in order to improve outcomes for children and young people (Greenfield, 2011). This integrated approach to working brings practitioners into contact with a range of practitioners from different disciplines and teams, for example, health, education and social services. This can cause barriers to communication, problems in understanding specialist knowledge and differing ways of working (Duffy and Marshall, 2007).

Wigfall and Moss (2001) in their study of a multi-agency setting identified several factors that appeared to be impeding the integration of the variety of health, social services and education services on offer. They found that there were external forces, that is government policy and agendas that appeared to be hampering coordinated work. They argued that these agendas and policies can work against effective networks when introducing too many initiatives, projects, targets, funding schemes and other mechanisms specific to particular services simultaneously. They also highlighted the lack of attention paid to the provision of non-contact time, time required for professional development, as well as that necessary to establish collaborative links between working groups and individuals. Another constraint was the idea of individual agendas of being busy. Though they were referring to multiple agencies, this also occurs within individual settings. Each member of staff has several responsibilities, and reconciling this myriad of priorities is a difficult task, as it can quite easily lead to tensions between members of staff.

The development of an effective team is an ongoing issue within the early years sector as the composition of teams changes when practitioners leave, gain promotion or retire, or as new practitioners join the team. Practitioners may join an existing team or a leader may be appointed as a head teacher to set up a new school and establish a new team. Forming a team is more than collecting a group of people together and calling them a team. For a team to work collaboratively in an effective way, a process of team formation needs to take place, and this can take time. Handy (1990) suggests a team moves through four stages of development until a team ethos has been established:

1. *Forming* – at this stage the team is beginning to find its identity. At first the team works as a group of individuals; as they begin to work together, the team members become familiar and comfortable with the others. The leader at this stage will be assessing the strengths and weaknesses of each team member.

2. *Storming* – this is the team development stage, through this stage there may be challenge and conflict between members. The team leader needs to manage the conflict effectively to help the team holistically develop. The team is moving towards a general consensus and agreed working practices.

3. *Norming* – the identity of the team is established, the team begins to feel more cohesive. The ways of working become established and supported. Issues or disagreements are raised openly and discussed between team members. The team leader and members feel comfortable with each other, there is a feeling of trust, members work cooperatively and they start to think like a team.

4. *Performing* – this is where individuals feel like part of a team. The team ethos is productive and supportive, everyone working collaboratively in a supportive way in the same direction. The leader at this stage supports, discusses, reflects and reviews with the team to consolidate and develop provision and practice.

Recent government initiatives such as the development of integrated practice, establishing early intervention teams and the establishment of Foundation Stage units in primary schools, have promoted the establishment of new teams. In creating a team culture it is essential that time and effort is spent in creating the conditions necessary for a collaborative climate to emerge. There is a need to develop partnerships among members of staff, which in turn requires the breaking down of rigid boundaries, the establishment of trust and respect between all those involved, in spite of differing qualifications and experience, and the potential of staff to work flexibly and share expertise.

In two different settings in the REPEY study, two teams from the nursery and reception class were merged together to form an early years unit. The following case study shows the formation of a new team.

Case study: Forming a new team

The following excerpts are taken from interviews with two lead nursery class teachers. Both their settings have seen the recent establishment of an early years unit, the amalgamation of the nursery and reception classes and the emergence of an early years coordinator. In both cases the assigned coordinator has been the reception teacher. Without much explanation, it is fairly easy to identify which teacher has come from a nursery where an effort has been made to ensure a genuine collaborative environment and which teacher has not.

The following comments were made in response to the question: do you think the Curriculum Guidance for the Early Years Foundation Stage has influenced your setting since it was introduced? The nursery teacher in charge of a nursery class in one setting responds:

> I would say that the activities that we have done haven't varied a great deal. The major difference is in the planning, in the actual pro formas we have been given, because we are now *having* to work with reception. Our coordinator is a reception teacher who, I don't think, has ever worked in a nursery before, and so she has tried to cobble the two ideas together … that has been the major influence on us; the planning, and losing our sort of, not individuality, but exclusiveness … We tend to do what we do in the nursery, and we think that the reception staff have to look for children's progression. They have all the details of our planning, they know exactly what goes on, they come in and visit us on occasion, and we talk about it if they want to know. In a sense, we start them off and then we hope that they will take it from there. We are not given access to their planning.

In response to the same question, the lead nursery teacher of a nursery class in another setting states:

> At present, the EYFS has not affected our practice a great deal. Apart from the fact that it's allowing us to work more closely with reception and thinking more for the whole Foundation Stage as opposed to only the nursery. Of course there was always a progression between the two – from nursery to reception – but it was very much them and us and we weren't working that closely together; whereas now we're making an effort to make the whole curriculum for the nursery children and the reception children and for us, as a nursery staff, and them, as a reception staff. And we've tried, together, to do our planning in that respect as well.

There are ways of establishing a team culture among staff, and the leader plays a key role in this process. The task is not easy; DuFour (2004) argues that it requires unrelenting commitment by the leader to promote the collaborative environment, despite the inevitable resistance she or he should anticipate encountering. Neugebauer and Neugebauer (1998) present a team-building process in five stages: set achievable goals, clarify roles within the team, build supportive relationships, encourage active participation and monitor team effectiveness. Effective team leadership and team-building results in high-quality interactions between team members and the leader. There is increased trust and openness in interpersonal relationships and shared understandings. A team approach supports professional development as experience and expertise is shared within the team (Rodd, 2013).

The leader of a nursery school in the next case study, from the REPEY study, demonstrates a clear commitment to the promotion of a team culture of collaboration and towards a learning community.

 ## Case study: Facilitating the development of a culture of collaboration

The head teacher of nursery school demonstrates a firm commitment to creating an atmosphere of collaboration among her members of staff, which in turn promotes the ongoing professional development of *all* staff members through an Inset [in-service training] programme and weekly staff meetings. In an effort to ensure that all staff have access to relevant professional development opportunities and are able to participate in an ongoing dialogue between one another, the head teacher has fought for and successfully organized the closure of the nursery school every Wednesday afternoon; this in spite of some expressed annoyance by parents, although it is important to note that this head teacher informed parents of this routine closure and its purpose prior to proceeding with their child's registration at the nursery. By closing the nursery school early, the head teacher was able to ensure that nursery nurses and support staff, along with full-time members of staff, such as nursery teachers, were able to participate within their working hours; therefore demonstrating an understanding of issues of status, as low-paid staff were not expected to remain after working hours.

These afternoon sessions are used for a variety of purposes, including reviewing and revising internal policies, updates about children, classroom practice and nursery school changes, introducing or reviewing external policies or mandated changes, and a variety of Inset days led either by a member of staff or by someone external to the nursery school. The staff are also given a set amount of time prior to the start of the day to discuss the day's plans and delegate

(Continues)

(Continued)

responsibilities. The head teacher explained that these morning sessions are attended by the team coordinator, with input from a senior staff member. There are also weekly 'pastoral meetings', which consist of the pastoral deputy visiting various teams to share issues around concerns about particular children.

Another important feature of this head teacher's commitment to developing a team culture among her staff is the process by which school policies are developed through collegial effort, as demonstrated in the following case study.

Case study: Collaborative school policy

All policies are created via consultation between leaders and members of staff. An initial discussion offers *all* members of staff an opportunity to contribute ideas and suggestions to improving or developing policies around issues such as behaviour, health and safety and curriculum. The ideas and suggestions that emerge during this initial session are then reflected upon, and where appropriate used, by the head teacher and deputy head of the nursery or relevant curriculum leader, who proceed to draft a written copy of the policy. This written draft is then presented to the staff for re-examination, discussion, amendment and finally approval before the policy is finalised as a document. This 'finalization' is regarded as temporary as the policies in this nursery school are returned to and reviewed regularly, either as part of their routine of review or in response to an environmental stimulus. Environmental stimulus might include an incident within the setting, for example, unmanageable behaviour of a child, which calls into question current behaviour management practice and requires reflection, discussion and modification of current policy and practice. The head teacher reflects upon the process of collaboratively developing school policies:

> If you have sat down as a staff and talked out a policy, really talked it through, where people raise questions, ask for clarification and suggest amendments or omissions based on observations or experiences, then you can be fairly certain that the policy and more importantly, the practice it intends to guide, will be understood with a deeper level of consistency, with those responsible for ensuring its implementation … the process is great. When we come to review we take the policy apart and we add bits and take bits away until we get it 'right' and then we argue it out some more.

The collaborative process of developing and writing a policy for a school, setting or children's centre is a reflective process of critical reflection, discussion and planning, experimentation and observation in implementation, and review. The process then begins again in a cyclical manner, as illustrated in Figure 5.1.

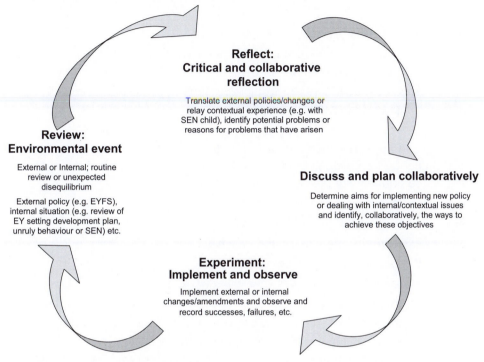

Reflect:
Critical and collaborative
reflection

Translate external policies/changes or relay contextual experience (e.g. with SEN child), identify potential problems or reasons for problems that have arisen

Review:
Environmental event

External or Internal; routine review or unexpected disequilibrium

External policy (e.g. EYFS), internal situation (e.g. review of EY setting development plan, unruly behaviour or SEN) etc.

Discuss and plan collaboratively

Determine aims for implementing new policy or dealing with internal/contextual issues and identify, collaboratively, the ways to achieve these objectives

Experiment:
Implement and observe

Implement external or internal changes/amendments and observe and record successes, failures, etc.

Figure 5.1 Policy development

In referring to the cycle of policy development above, use the following reflective questions to help you reflect upon your leadership of policy development or, your involvement in developing policy. Consider your collaborative leadership or the level of collaborative involvement you experienced.

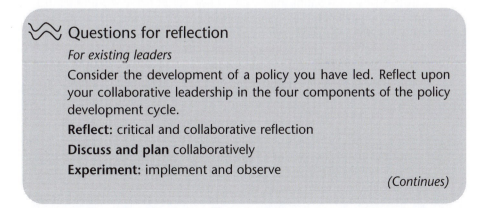

〰 Questions for reflection

For existing leaders

Consider the development of a policy you have led. Reflect upon your collaborative leadership in the four components of the policy development cycle.

Reflect: critical and collaborative reflection

Discuss and plan collaboratively

Experiment: implement and observe

(Continues)

(Continued)

Review: environmental event

- How collaborative was your leadership?
- How do you know, you involved contributions from all members of staff?
- What was the outcome?
- How effective was your collaboration and how is it demonstrated in the implementation of the policy?
- Is there anything you would do differently in leading the development of another policy?

For aspiring leaders

Consider the development of a policy you have been involved in. Reflect upon your experience of collaborative leadership in the four components of the policy development cycle.

Reflect: critical and collaborative reflection

Discuss and plan collaboratively

Experiment: implement and observe

Review: environmental event

- How collaborative was your experience?
- How do you know, your contribution was included in the policy?
- How effective was your experience of collaboration and how is it demonstrated in the implementation of the policy?
- Is there anything you learnt from this experience of policy development to include in your own collaborative leadership?

 Summary

The chapter discussed collaborative leadership and the leadership practice of developing and promoting a team culture to build and sustain positive relationships in a school, setting or children's centre in which reflective dialogue can take place. The discussion is illustrated with a range of case studies showing collaborative leadership, teamwork and collaboratively leading the development of policy. Questions for reflection enable leaders and aspiring leaders to consider their collaborative leadership and promote a team culture.

The next chapter continues discussion about *collaborative leadership* and examines the leadership practice of *promoting parental collaboration* within an early years setting, children's centre or school.

Further reading 📖

Blatchford, P., Russell, A., Bassett, P., Brown, P. and Martin, C. (2007) 'The role and effects of teaching assistants in English primary schools', *British Educational Research Journal*, 33(1): 5–26.

This journal article includes a discussion about the working relationship between teaching assistants and teachers and deployment in the classroom so they can be used effectively to help teachers and pupils.

Bush, T. and Middlewood, D. (2013) *Leading and Managing People in Education*. 3rd edn. London: Sage. pp. 124–42.

Chapter 8 in this book, 'Leading and managing through teams' explains the rationale for teamwork, discusses the advantages and disadvantages of teamwork, and considers the composition of leadership and management teams in several countries with examples of teamwork in New Zealand and England.

Greenfield, S. (2011) 'Working in multidisciplinary teams', in L. Miller and C. Cable (eds), *Professionalization, Leadership and Management in the Early Years*. London: Sage. pp. 77–90.

Chapter 3 in this book explores ways that professionals from different backgrounds work together in multi-disciplinary teams.

Jones, C. and Pound, L. (2008) *Leadership and Management in the Early Years*. Maidenhead: Open University Press. pp. 25–43.

Chapter 3 in this book, 'Leader of leaders: developing a team culture' discusses further the leadership role of developing a team.

Leeson, C. and Huggins, V. (2010) 'Working with colleagues', in R. Parker-Rees, C. Leeson, J. Willan and J. Savage (eds), Early Childhood Studies, 4th edn. Exeter: Learning Matters. pp. 101–11.

Chapter 8 in this book explores some key issues in effective collaboration with colleagues.

Collaborative leadership: promoting parental collaboration

Chapter overview

The leadership practice of *promoting parental collaboration* within the *collaborative leadership* theme is explored in this chapter. The chapter discusses the importance of promoting collaborative involvement of parents in their child's early education, learning and development; and the role leaders of early years settings, schools and children's centres can play in encouraging this involvement and promoting a partnership between parents and staff. Case studies illustrate examples of leaders collaboratively working with parents. There is opportunity for reflection about promoting parental collaboration. The inclusive term 'parent' refers to children's parent or parents, carers and guardians.

This chapter will:

- consider the importance of collaborative involvement of parents and partnership working for children, families and practitioners

- explore ways of promoting parental collaboration

- reflect upon leaders' experiences of collaborative leadership in partnership working with parents

- provide opportunity for professional reflection about parental collaboration.

Reciprocity: home and early years settings

Evidence demonstrates that consistency across home and early years settings, between parents and early years staff, promotes happiness and achievement for young children (Sylva et al., 2004). Despite this evidence base, the relationship between home and an early years setting, school or children's centre generally remains unilateral, with the direction of information about children moving from the early years setting and staff to the parents, and rarely in the opposite direction. With the widening range of services revolving around children and their families, such as health services, social care and education, there is a growing need and expectation for the development of partnerships with parents and families and reciprocity in sharing of information.

In the early years sector, there have been several government mandates attempting to ensure the forging of this relationship between home and school. In the Early Years Foundation Stage (EYFS) curriculum framework, parents are recognized as the child's first educator (DCSF, 2008b). In the Tickell Review of the EYFS, Tickell (2011) recommends involvement of parents and carers or their nominee in providing information about their child along with other professionals such as speech and language therapists. Parents are to be encouraged to enter information in their child's early childhood health record, known as the Red Book, on an inserted record sheet. Nutbrown (2012), in her review of early education and childcare qualifications, highlights the positive impact that working effectively with parents can have on children. She recommends students in their early years and childcare training learn how to work effectively with families and share information with parents and carers in a reciprocal way. Similarly, practitioners should learn how to regard parents as experts on their own children, to listen and to learn from them, supporting each child's well-being, learning and development. There is a range of ways of working collaboratively with families including holding one-to-one conversations, arranging events to share information, and visiting families in their homes as part of transition, early intervention and family support programmes (Nutbrown, 2012).

In the following case study, an early years leader explains ways of sharing information with parents when starting school, and how she involves parents in children's literacy learning.

 ## Case study: Involving parents

Elena is the Reception Team Leader in the open-plan base of a primary school. She works with Mary, another reception teacher, and Sue the nursery nurse. There are two classes and 60 children in the base. Elena reflects upon her leadership, educational philosophy, pedagogy and practice about children starting school and working with parents in language and literacy learning.

When a child starts school, I also believe that the parent, parents

(Continues)

(Continued)

and carers, and extended family such as grandparents, begin school too. The child leaves the familiar home environment to join a larger and unfamiliar one. The transition from one environment to another should be as gradual and smooth as possible for the child and their parent or parents. I raised the issue of transition at a weekly planning meeting, and with my two team members and the staff from the nursery unit, I led the discussion. By listening to others and valuing their experience, expertise and ideas, we collaboratively developed a range of activities to inform and involve parents in their children's transition from home and nursery to school with a focus on early literacy learning:

• a transition programme

• a language workshop

• a literacy library.

The *transition programme* is a series of meetings giving information to parents about their child's school experience and to meet staff their child will be working with, particularly their child's key person. At one meeting, there is an opportunity for parents to experience some activities their children will be doing; the base is set up with activities, parents are able to paint, play, draw, investigate, problem solve and add up. There is plenty of time for parents to ask questions of any member of staff; the start of building positive relationships begins. The home visit in which the child's reception teacher and key person visit the parent and child in their home, also begins to forge relationships between parents, staff and children. The children have a series of visits to the reception class from the nursery unit or their home in the half term prior to starting school. These visits develop in length and time to include new and unfamiliar routines such as play time, dinner time, story time and a Physical Education (PE) session in the hall.

The development of language and literacy is a key that unlocks the curriculum. I wanted to involve parents in supporting their child's literacy and language learning. For an hour each morning, the reception base becomes a *language workshop*. Tables are set out, one for each child. A folder with their name on is laid on the table, inside it is a collection of resources to inspire and encourage their language, reading and writing. There is a story book and associated puppet or toy. There is a non-fiction book connected to the story, a language game based upon the story book to play and a suggestion for a story to write based on an aspect of the book. There is an information sheet for parents with instructions how to use each resource.

(Continued)

I appreciate that working parents are unable to attend the language workshops so I set up a *literacy library*, a collection of plastic folders holding resources, activities and instructions to develop reading and writing in the home. One of the folders contains a DVD of a story about Postman Pat to watch and listen to, and the story book *The Jolly Postman* by Janet and Allan Alhberg, a selection of writing paper, envelopes and a pen with the invitation to write a letter to a friend, relative, teacher or a soft toy. A trip or walk to post the letter encourages the child to draw a map of their route to the post office, so developing geographical knowledge and understanding of their local neighbourhood. The folders in the literacy library are borrowed by children to share with their parents, carers, sisters and brothers, extended family of grandparents, aunts and uncles in the home.

I am the Language and Literacy Coordinator with responsibility to lead language and literacy pedagogy and provision throughout the primary school. These literacy initiatives have started in the reception base, with ongoing review and evaluation. I shared my findings at a whole-school staff meeting, and they were met with interest. I'm now going to work with the teaching team in the next class to develop a language workshop suitable for the age group they teach. The aim is for language workshops to develop appropriately for each age group throughout the school.

The following question will help you reflect upon how you promote parental collaboration through your leadership.

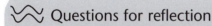 Questions for reflection

For existing leaders

Consider and reflect upon how you have led parental collaboration and involvement in your setting, school or children's centre.

- What aspect of parental collaboration have you led?
- How do you know this has been effective for parents?
- How do you know this has been effective for children?
- How do you know this has been effective for staff?
- What have you learnt about leading and promoting parental collaboration?
- As a leader would you do anything differently in the future?

(Continues)

For aspiring leaders

Consider and reflect upon your involvement in promoting parental collaboration and involvement in your setting, school or children's centre.

- What aspect of parental collaboration have you been involved in?
- How do you know this has been effective for parents?
- How do you know this has been effective for children?
- How do you know this has been effective for staff?
- What have you learnt about leading and promoting parental collaboration?
- As an aspiring leader would you do anything differently?

Parental partnership

In the early years, primary and secondary sectors, there have been several initiatives to promote parental collaboration and partnership working. One of the main objectives of *Every Child Matters* (DfES, 2004b), a cross-sector initiative, was to ensure the improvement of the level and degree of support offered to parents and carers, including increased universal services providing information and advice, as well as specialist support if and when required. The Allen Review (2011) furthers parental collaboration and partnership working through early intervention programmes. The aim is promoted and upheld by the view that parents, carers and families are the most important influence on children and young people's outcomes (DfES, 2004b).

This is supported by much of the literature on parental participation in children's learning and education. There are several studies which highlight family and parent involvement in children's learning as having an influence on their achievement and learning in schools (Arvizu, 1996; Nutbrown et al., 2005; Sylva et al., 2010). There is evidence which demonstrates that this partnership can also improve children's motivation, behaviour and self-esteem. Desforges and Abouchaar (2003) concur that parental involvement in schools and early years settings and, above all, the educational environment of the home, have a positive effect on children's achievement and adjustment.

Wolfendale (1992) claims that parents are their child's prime educators, something supported by more recent work from Sylva et al. (2004). Their research in the EPPE project found that work with parents as first educators is an effective strategy, as a child's home learning environment has a significant impact upon children's learning and development. Sylva et al. (2004) argue that intervening with parents in early childhood has powerful effects on language, cognition and self-esteem, particularly for 3- and 4-year-old children. Allen (2011), in his review of early intervention, recommends providing parents with the information and support they need to help their children, that is, providing multi-professional resources for intervention, early in a child's life rather than later on. He highlights what parents do is more important than who they are, in socio-economic terms. Especially in their earliest years, the right kind of parenting has more influence on a child's future than wealth, class, education or any other common social factor.

Initiatives to involve parents have, therefore, ranged in intention from compensatory to the active promotion of parent rights. Epstein (1986) offers a useful typology of parent involvement and identifies five types of parental involvement: parenting skills, child development and home environment for learning; communications between school, early years setting, children's centre and home; parents as volunteers in school, setting and children's centre; parents' involvement in their children's learning at home; and parental involvement in decision-making, leadership and governance.

Home–school initiatives in the past three decades have been many and varied, and have changed from being largely compensatory in nature to participatory, collaborative and inclusive of parents, schools, settings, children's centres and children. Parent involvement has been interpreted in a number of ways, such as: parents working as volunteers in schools, settings, children's centres and in extended schools services, such as after-school clubs (Vincent, 2012). Parents as educators at home, and parents as governors in the management of schools, can provide a forum for the 'parent voice', bringing the lay or non-professional perspective to educational services (Vincent, 2012: 24).

The term 'parental partnership' is commonly used, but what is meant by this term? Pugh and Duffy (2010) found that when parents and practitioners work together the results have a positive impact on children's learning and development. The starting point is the belief that all parents are interested in the development and progress of their child (Whalley and Pen Green Team, 2008). Parental partnership is a working relationship that is characterized by a shared sense of purpose, mutual respect and a willingness to negotiate. This implies a sharing of information, responsibility, skills, decision-making and accountability (Pugh and Duffy, 2010). Partnership working is based upon equality; neither partner has more power in the relationship than the other (Hallet, 2013). The quality of relationships formed is central to the effectiveness of parental partnership, but this takes time to nurture and establish through respect and trust (Draper and Duffy, 2010).

Initiatives to involve parents have ranged in intention from compensatory to the active promotion of parent rights. Foot et al. (2002) attempt to define the term 'partnership'. They argue partnership goes beyond involvement; it is not just including parents in support and activities of pre-school education. Partnership implies equality and a division of power which inevitably draws parents into decision-making and policy issues, not merely helping and information-sharing. It moves towards an empowerment of parents and increasing their self-efficacy. Foot et al. (2002) argue that the types of involvement on offer to parents should not be limited to activities which *directly* promote the children or the 'school', but also towards making parents the direct recipients of their involvement. Such active participation in attending, for instance, courses offered, planned or advertised by an early years setting, children's centre or school can promote parents' self-efficacy, which can make parents conscious of their influential role over their child's development and therefore improve interactions with their children and the activities they provide when children are in their care. Whalley and the Pen Green Team (2008) refer to the parents in their study as having their own proper competences and expertise. Genuine recognition of the very real contribution parents can make in their child's life both inside and outside the home requires a level of open, reciprocal and non-hierarchical communication.

That said, the level of variation in the way the concept 'parental partnership' is envisaged and promoted by schools and settings is considerable. In interviews conducted with parents in the REPEY study there were disparities among parents within settings in terms of their knowledge and awareness of opportunities and information offered by the settings their children attended. This discrepancy might suggest that the pre-school setting needs to ensure, via self-evaluation checks, that channels of communication are clear and available to all parents, although evidence in many of the settings seems to suggest that attempts to ensure this clarity of communication with parents is already in place. For instance, in one pre-school, staff ensure that parents who are unable to attend open meetings receive minutes summarizing the information disseminated and decisions taken, in several community languages as well as English. That said, the discrepancy might suggest a different limitation. A parent from another setting, pleased with the level of communication provided by the private day nursery her child was attending, highlights an interesting alternative argument regarding the importance of shared responsibility between home and school: 'I think it's also up to the parents; you cannot expect the nursery staff to spoon feed you. Parents have to take an active interest in finding out what's on offer.'

Leading parental collaboration

With the growing importance placed upon the involvement of parents in children's education and development, it is essential that early years leaders evaluate their current home–school policy to reflect collaborative partnership working with parents, an equal and active dialogue between parents and early childhood educators (Whalley and Pen Green Team, 2008). It is only through this reciprocity and recognition of the mutual benefit that both parties, parents and early years staff, can contribute to children's learning and development that we will realize the true benefits of promoting this collaborative relationship and partnership working.

A strong connection between families and early years providers is essential for providing quality learning environments for children. Identified in the StartRight (Ball, 1994) report, the role of the early years setting is to support parents through exemplifying good practice, providing information about current research, offering appropriate parent education and professional support, and helping parents to develop and sustain their sense of self-esteem and self-efficacy. Parental involvement and courses for parents form a core part of early childhood services, particularly in SureStart children's centres which offer a range of parenting courses. Rodd (2013: 222) highlights three common themes in parental involvement and parenting classes: *partnership* – a philosophy of shared child-rearing; *continuity* – the promotion of consistency between the conditions and experience of the home and the setting, school or children's centre; and *parent education* – the professional responsibility to support and educate parents to enhance children's well-being, parental enjoyment and the parenting role.

Parents are not a homogeneous group and therefore can hold differing culturally conceived ideas and understanding about education, teachers, educators and their role as parent educators. In some cultures the role of the 'teacher' is seen as quite distinct and separate to the role of parenting. In the following case study, vignettes from the REPEY study demonstrate ways settings have informed and involved parents about their child's education, learning and development through several ways of parental education.

 ## Case study: Parental education

Settings with good and successful outcomes provided regular information through records of achievement and monthly meetings with key persons, and weekly feedback is provided. What is distinctive about all of these settings is that they focus on what they are teaching the children and report regularly on the children's achievements, offering the opportunity for consistency of learning opportunities between home and school. These settings engage in more regular ongoing assessment of children's learning, and this supports the parents from these settings in engaging more in complementary educational activities in the home.

We had an induction meeting for parents and the teachers went

(Continues)

(Continued)

> through everything with us, I know they are assessing as they go on and it's continual assessment. They were going to let us know how our child performed it's not a standard test but they're watching them. They were going to let us know what stage they're at but I'm not quite sure what form that's going to take whether it's a meeting or a written report.

Parents from these settings are proactive in initiating learning activities at home. Where this was combined with staff encouraging positive dispositions, such as independence, the children often led and initiated the learning activities at home themselves. One nursery class in particular really emphasized peer sociability and had a strong consistent policy of engaging children in discussion, as this parent reflects:

> Before when he first came here we had just started to get him to write his name. A lot of letters were around the wrong way and he was missing out a letter. I don't know if what we do at home is supported by the nursery, I think it is initiated by the nursery. As soon as he came here he changed, in that he wanted to be able to achieve, the children are very independent and meant to be, I saw the need when he came home for me to teach him how to do things. So that when he was at nursery he was doing similar things so it was not a problem.

By providing some examples of ways early years leaders in these settings respond to promoting the development of a parental partnership, several implications for practitioners are revealed:

> Sometimes parents will want to know why we're doing things in a particular way but they seem to be quite happy with the explanations. And I think part of that is because when our parents are first introduced to the nursery we see them half a term before their children start. And during that time we explain our philosophy and we try to demonstrate some of the ethos of the nursery by inviting them in for visits so that they can see the children working. And we say to them 'look the children are doing science and it looks like this'; 'the children here are doing maths, but it looks like this'.

This particular early years leader goes on to explain how she uses examples in an effort to make clear the nursery's approaches and activities:

> One of the things I tend to do is use as an example some sort of art activity that we will expect small children to be doing and then show how cross-curricular that is. By saying that while they're doing it they're talking to each other, they may be painting a picture of their family, what they're wearing, what their clothes are made of, whether granny and grandad are there then you're talking history. We just try to explain it to parents like that. To say that this is the

seed of all these other things that children are going to experience later.

Parents are offered genuine opportunity to get the necessary support. By providing parents with this service and time away from their child, the staff inadvertently legitimizes the process of parental support. A large parents' room is available for groups and meetings. A parenting group meets weekly, led by multi-agency professionals from a nearby health centre. The nursery staff runs a crèche while the parents talk and receive advice. Also, on open evenings, when parents are invited into the nursery class, the staff put out appropriate toys for the younger siblings of centre children who usually attend.

The partnership approach to parental involvement stresses a cooperative, collaborative approach to working together, rather than a joint activity. In this approach, parents are able to decide upon their level of commitment in terms of other work and family commitments. The Pen Green Centre in Corby and the Reggio Emilia pre-schools in northern Italy are examples where parents and practitioners have engaged in strong partnerships that are empowering for both parties and benefit children's learning and development (Abbott and Nutbrown, 2001). Such working partnerships are based on equal but different contributions, shared accountability and responsibility (Rodd, 2013). This begins with early years leaders' commitment to parental involvement and collaborative working, and for this pedagogy to be included in policy for practice. A coordinator for parental involvement to lead policy and monitor practice may be created.

The case study below is an example from the REPEY study of an early years leader implementing an approach to listening to parents' voices.

 Case study: Parents' voices

The early years leader from a private nursery regularly reviews parental attitudes by using questionnaires to ascertain parents' and carers' opinions over a wide range of relevant issues. The questionnaire is issued to enable parents to express their opinions, and several parents mention this practice as an effective conduit to influence and effect changes, for example, menus and security issues. Parents were asked to comment upon the following:

(Continues)

(Continued)

- the level of welcome offered by staff and setting
- whether the time provided for parents to communicate with staff was sufficient
- the ease of access to the senior leader
- dissemination of information about the educational programme, procedures and routines and safety
- the relevance and usefulness of the information disseminated, for example, the newsletter
- staff attitudes
- opportunities for consultation
- value for money (fees)
- menus
- other issues concerning general satisfaction.

The questionnaire requires parents to rate each of the above from 0 to 10 with a space provided to include any ideas for improvement or general comments. The questionnaires are then gathered, the information collated and presented to the staff to facilitate discussion and identify points for action, and this information is then fed back to parents. This method of testing and responding to parental opinion provides very strong support and protection against national and local authority requirements and standards, especially as the invited anonymity suggests invoking truthful responses. A parent reflects upon her involvement:

> We have a questionnaire we're asked to fill in that allows us to offer any suggestions or note any concerns; of course we can include the things we are pleased with as well. We always get feedback from that. When all the questionnaires have been gathered and the information's been collated you get it back. One year, menus came up, parents commented about the variety of food the children had and they tried to change the menus. In that sense we were involved. I read in one of the newsletters that they are looking at having some kind of meeting for the parents of the children who are going to the primary school. We could comment on the curriculum and the activities children do if we wanted. You always feel you'd be listened to.

The case studies in this chapter have provided a range of ways of working with parents in a collaborative way. The following questions give opportunity for existing leaders to consider leading parental involvement in a collaborative way, or for aspiring leaders to reflect upon their involvement in working with parents.

Questions for reflection

For existing leaders

Reflect upon a way you have led an aspect of parental involvement. Write a short narrative to describe this.

- Do you consider you led in a collaborative way? If so, how was this achieved? If not, why?
- Do you consider that you worked in equal partnership with parents? If so, how was this achieved?
- How did you know the partnership was effective? What were the benefits for the parents, the children, the practitioners, other stakeholders?
- In considering your collaborative leadership in promoting parental collaboration. What have you learnt about your leadership? What would you do differently?

For aspiring leaders

Reflect upon a way you have been involved in an aspect of parental involvement. Write a short narrative to describe this.

- Do you consider it was collaborative between parents and practitioners? If so, how was this achieved? If not, why?
- Do you consider that there was an equal partnership between parents and practitioners? If so, how was this achieved? If not, why?
- Do you consider that the aspect of parental involvement was collaboratively led? If so, how was this achieved? If not, why?
- How did you know the partnership was effective?
- What were the benefits for parents, children, practitioners and other stakeholders?
- In considering leading and promoting parental collaboration, what have you learnt about collaborative leadership and, as a leader, how would you promote parental collaboration?

 Summary

This chapter has explored ways of promoting parental collaboration within the collaborative leadership theme. The importance of promoting collaborative involvement and working in partnership with parents in their child's early education, at home, at transition, and in a setting, children's centre and school is discussed and illustrated through examples of leadership practice. There is opportunity for leaders and aspiring leaders to reflect upon working with parents and leading in parental involvement in a collaborative way.

→ The next chapter defines the third leadership theme, *empowering leadership* in effective and caring leadership practices in the early years, examining the leadership practice of *promoting agency in others.*

Further reading

Clarkin-Phillips, J. and Carr, M. (2012) 'An affordance network for engagement: increasing parent and family agency in an early childhood education setting', *European Early Childhood Education Research Journal*, 20(2): 177–87.
This journal article describes an initiative from New Zealand about leadership in an early childhood centre in the implementation of integrated services, the establishment of a playgroup for parents and caregivers with babies and toddlers. The authors analyse the impact by applying the notion of an affordance network for engagement opportunities and increasing the possibilities of agency for families.

Dockett, S. and Perry, B. (2012) '"In kindy you don't get taught": continuity and change as children start school', *Frontiers of Education in China*, 7(1): 5–32.
This journal article explores young Australian children's perceptions of school and learning, as expressed through drawings and conversations about school.

Needham, M. and Jackson, D. (2012) 'Stay and play or play and chat: comparing roles and purposes in case studies of English and Australian supported playgroups', *European Early Childhood Education Research Journal*, 20(2): 163–76.
The journal article considers the extent to which Australian Supported Playgroups and English Parent–Toddler groups might be similar activities by considering the purpose of the groups from parents' and practitioners' perspectives.

Neumann, M. M. and Neumann, D.L. (2010) 'Parental strategies to scaffold emergent writing skills in the pre-school child within the home environment', *Early Years*, 30(1): 79–94.
This journal article describes research from Australia about joint writing activities between parent and child that can enhance literacy skills in young children.

O'Conner, A. (2013) *Understanding Transitions in the Early Years: supporting change through attachment and resilience.* Abingdon: Routledge.
This book explains the importance of transitions and provides practical guidance in how to support young children in many transitions including the significant transition from home to an early years setting.

Rodd, J. (2013) 'Building shared understanding with parents and the public', in J. Rodd (ed.). *Leadership in Early Childhood*, 3rd edn. Maidenhead: Open University Press. pp. 219–42.
Chapter 12 in this book further discusses challenges and approaches to leading and working collaboratively with parents.

7

Empowering leadership: promoting agency in others

Chapter overview

The theme *empowering leadership* in effective and caring leadership in the early years is defined and the leadership practice of *promoting agency in others* discussed. A leader's ability to influence and empower others to lead is a central leadership practice. Through distributed, shared and transformative leadership, this leadership practice builds individual leadership capability and capacity within an organization and for the future development of it.

This chapter will:

- consider the importance for a leader to influence others, empowering them for confident agency in leading others and an organization

- explore ways of developing leadership capability and agency through influence, and through transformative, distributed and shared leadership

- reflect upon experiences of empowering leadership practice.

Influencing leadership

Rodd (2013) offers a fairly detailed workable definition of leadership, one which attempts to identify the complexity of the leader's role. Leadership can be described as a process by which one person sets certain standards and expectations and influences the actions of others to behave in what is considered a desirable manner. Leaders are people who can influence the behaviour of others for the purpose of achieving a goal. Leaders possess a special set of somewhat elusive qualities and skills which are combined into an ability to get others to do what the leader wants because they want to do it. Leaders are able to balance the concern for work, task, quality and productivity with concern for people, relationships, satisfaction and morale. They combine an orientation towards innovation and change with an interest in continuity and stability for the present. They do this by using personal qualities which command respect and promote feelings of trust and security. They are also responsible for setting and clarifying goals, roles and responsibilities, collecting information, planning, making decisions and involving members of the group by communicating, encouraging and acknowledging commitment and contribution.

Influential leaders empower others and develop leaders' agency to improve organizations and develop their leadership practice. This leadership know-ledge, quality, skill and behaviour is reflected in one of the standards, in the *National Standards for Leaders of SureStart Children's Centres*, 'Shaping the present and creating the future' and for children's centre leaders to 'identify and promote the development of potential future centre leaders (DCSF, 2007: 13). The contribution of influence in leadership is further developed in the 'Draft national standards for leadership of SureStart children's centre services' (Siraj-Blatchford and Hallet, 2012: 12) in the 'Leading people and effective teams' standard; children's centre leaders are required to develop, inspire and motivate individuals and teams, recognizing and deploying their strengths, and act as an authentic role model' influencing others within, across and beyond the services within their children's centre and wider children's services.

A central element in many definitions of leadership is that there is a process of influence (Bush and Glover, 2003) whereby intentional influence is exerted individually or by a group or a team over individuals, structuring activities and relationships in a group or organization (Yukl, 2002). Influencing leadership may be individual or team leadership. The following reflection from an early years leader in the LLEaP project shows the importance of motivation and influencing behaviour in her leadership practice.

 ## Case study: Leader's reflection – influencing leadership

Sam is a playgroup leader in a community-based playgroup held in a church hall. Reflecting upon her influencing leadership practice, she commented:

I see myself as a '*worker ant*', someone who is constantly seeking to bring inspiration, new ideas, and help others in their practice. I have learnt to listen to others and I have encouraged them to come in with their own ideas. Leadership is only as good as the motivation it gives to others and the value placed on others. The playgroup is the people in the playgroup, everyone is valued and involved, their thoughts, ideas and strengths are used to bring out the best combination. They are all play-leaders and influence the activities we do with the children and families. Some will set up an activity and take a lead, we learn from each other and share ideas.

If I visit another playgroup and seen an interesting activity, I will try it out with the children, and share it with the others. By demonstrating and influencing, I develop and support practice. Last week, I went to a neighbouring playgroup, the play-leaders were in the local park, playing parachute games with the children. The children were running *in* and *out*, *through* and *under* the parachute, the play-leaders made the parachute go *up* and *high* in the air and *low* and *down* onto the ground. The children were being physically active and having fun outdoors.

With my educator's hat on, the activity was helping their mathematical understanding, they were experiencing mathematical language in a physical and healthy way. I borrowed the parachute for a day and played similar games with children in the field at the back of our playgroup. The colourful parachute was a magnet to the children, and the play-leaders were intrigued by the play resource. One by one, I showed them the various games you could do with a parachute. By the end of the day, all the play-leaders had played parachute games with the children. I had to take the parachute back. At our next staff meeting, we evaluated the parachute activity and the learning experience it provided for children. I shared my thoughts about the mathematical language and understanding the children experienced through the parachute games. Through discussion, the play-leaders decided they would like a parachute as a resource for outdoor learning in our playgroup. I'm finding out the price of a parachute, putting a proposal to purchase a parachute to the playgroup committee to discuss at the next meeting. On reflection about my leadership practice, I led by demonstration, having knowledge and understanding of young children's mathematical learning and influenced through working with, and leading the play-leaders.

The ability for a leader to promote agency and influence others is a key attribute in transformational leadership. The characteristics and attributes of transformational leadership are now discussed.

Transformational leadership

Transformational leadership is a process by which a leader fosters individual, group or organizational performance beyond expectation through strong emotional attachment and relationships. Transformational leaders both influence and are influenced by followers; they not only lead but also develop leaders (Diaz-Saenz, 2011). A transformational leader seems more likely to take actions that will empower followers and make them partners in a quest to achieve vision and important goals (Yukl, 1999). Transformational leadership is multi-dimensional, Bass (1985) identified four leadership behaviours in transformational leadership:

- idealized influence

- inspirational motivation

- intellectual stimulation

- individualized consideration.

Leaders with idealized influence become role models that others want to follow and even emulate. Leaders, who create inspirational motivation, form a clear vision and pathway through which they inspire and enable a team to achieve the vision. Leaders who show intellectual stimulation encourage others to be innovative and creative, addressing and solving problems in new ways and examining existing assumptions. Leaders who show individual consideration are concerned with each follower as an individual, considering their individual needs, abilities and aspirations, helping individuals to develop their strengths through coaching, guiding and mentoring (Diaz-Saenz, 2011).

Effective leaders transform or change the basic values, beliefs and attitudes of followers so they are willing to perform beyond the minimum levels specified by the organization (Podsakoff et al., 1990). The case study 'Cultivating leadership' later in this chapter demonstrates the effect of a transformative leader who cultivates her staff's leadership practices, through inspirational influence, so they developed personal and professional confidence, leadership knowledge, understanding and skills, and progressed in their leadership journey and career, eventually leaving the school to take on leadership roles in other organizations. Leaders who create inspirational motivation map out a clear vision for their followers' future state as well as developing a team spirit. Leaders showing individual consideration treat each of their followers as an individual by considering their individual needs, abilities and aspirations. They help individuals to develop their strengths and spend time coaching and guiding people (Diaz-Saenz, 2011). Six leadership behaviours and measures associated with the multi-dimensional nature of transformational leadership are identified by Podsakoff et al. (1990: 112) and illustrated in Figure 7.1.

Research into the use and effectiveness of transformational leadership in national cultural contexts (Den Hartog et al., 1999) found that aspects of transformative leadership are used internationally. Leadership behaviour is culturally situated. Depending upon the culture, the transformational

Identifying and articulating a vision
Behaviour on the part of the leader aimed at identifying new opportunities for his or her unit/division/company, and developing, articulating and inspiring others with his or her vision of the future

Providing an appropriate model
Behaviour on the part of the leader that sets an example for employees to follow that is consistent with the values the leader espouses

Fostering the acceptance of group goals
Behaviour on the part of the leader aimed at promoting cooperation among employees and getting them to work together towards a common goal

High performance expectations
Behaviour that demonstrates the leader's expectations for excellence, quality and/or high performance on the part of the followers

Providing individualized support
Behaviour on the part of the leader that indicates that he/she respects followers and is concerned about their personal feelings and needs. Supporting leadership development and professional learning for career progression

Intellectual stimulation
Behaviour on the part of the leader that challenges followers to re-examine some of their assumptions and rethink how leadership can be performed

Figure 7.1 Transformational leadership behaviours (adapted from Podsakoff et al., 1990: 112)

leadership relationship will be stronger within less traditional and more liberal western cultures such as the USA and the UK, and perceived as a weaker leadership style in cultures with a traditional culture such as Taiwan where hierarchy is respected. A collectivistic culture such as in Korea was found to enhance the transformational leadership effect, facilitating the follower's motivation to work for the collective group rather than self-interest (Jung et al., 2009) in a more individualist society such as the USA (Diaz-Saenz, 2011).

The contribution of transformational leadership to influence and empower others to lead in early childhood is important in building leadership capability within the workforce and for the sustainability of the setting, school, centre or service. This approach to organization and workforce sustainability is now considered.

Building leadership capability

An understanding and expectation of how leadership is performed is informed by images we and others have of the child, childhood and the construct of our professional self and identity. The traditional image of early childhood practitioners being caring, capable women caring for untroubled children gives an outdated 'Mary Poppins' image of women undertaking a perceived passive nurturing and caring role (Woodrow and Busch, 2008: 89) rather than a confident and active leadership role.

The evolving relationship between professionalism and leadership nationally and internationally (Miller and Cable, 2008) develops the concept of an 'activist professional' who has active engagement with others, across boundaries of professional, parent and community (Woodrow and Busch, 2008: 90). An activist identity is built on democratic principles and is negotiated, collaborative, socially critical, future orientated, strategic and tactical (Groundwater-Smith and Sachs, 2002). The construct of 'leadership-in-action' (Woodrow and Busch, 2008: 91) emerges; a new kind of leadership that is situated, local, crossing traditional professional boundaries such as health, social and educational. This Australian construct aligns with emerging professionalism and professional identity, leadership with professional and political agency for action, change and improvement of children's services.

The characteristic passion that early childhood practitioners express and practise in their work with children and families (Moyles, 2001) is a motivating power for practitioners' agency in their everyday work and leadership. Passion was identified as key driver in graduate early years leaders' practice to influence and inspire others (Hallet, 2014). The understanding of leadership as 'situated action' encourages early childhood practitioners to view themselves as leaders (Woodrow and Busch, 2008: 90).

Leadership in early childhood schools, settings, centres and services is contextually situated (Siraj-Blatchford and Manni, 2007); often pre-school settings are small in size and in staffing ratio. Situated leadership is constructed within the social and cultural context, and involves relationships with others (Woodrow and Busch, 2008). The notion of inclusive leadership promotes collaborative working through effective relationships (Rodd, 2013). Shared and inclusive leadership gives practicality to a small staff team, providing all aspects of provision for children and families which a sole leader would find difficult to provide. By developing a leaderful team (Raelin, 2003) in setting, school, centre or service grows early childhood leadership capacity and capability grow from within. Organizations survive and thrive not because of the leader, but as they cultivate leadership through the system (Goleman, 2002). In the next case study, an early years leader reflects upon her experience of working in a primary school with a head teacher who cultivated leadership capability in her staff.

Case study: Leader's reflection – cultivating leadership

Reeana is a recently appointed head teacher of a newly built primary school. She is enjoying the challenge of setting up a new school with policies, provision and practices with her staff team. She is developing an inclusive and democratic leadership style, wanting staff to contribute, develop and 'own' the policies that form provision and practice in the school. She asked herself, 'How have I got to this leadership position? Why am I developing this leadership style? Being inclusive and democratic takes time to listen to all views and develop policy, it would be much easier for me to be an autocratic leader and say, this is what we are doing!'

She reflected upon her own experience of inclusive leadership when working with a head teacher of a large primary school. The comment she heard many times from teachers outside the school, 'Oh if you work at ABC school, you always get on, loads of head and deputy teachers in the authority worked there' was similar to her own experience. Six teachers started working at the school at the same time as Reeana; after four years, five out of the six are now in leadership roles as head teachers, the other works in a university as a programme leader for a Foundation Degree in Early Childhood. The head teacher, Chris, had an inclusive and empowering leadership style. She identified expertise, strengths and leadership potential of her staff, provided opportunity for them to lead curriculum and staff, supported by professional development opportunities and recognition of the role and responsibility they held.

> She gave me an opportunity to lead and to develop my leadership knowledge, understanding and skills. To develop a creative approach to curriculum pedagogy, the school held an Arts Week, the usual timetable was suspended for a week and creative activities for children to engage in were provided by parents and staff. This meant the development of an Arts Week programme. The head teacher asked me from the infant department and Paul from the junior department to do this. We were both classroom teachers. At first, I thought why me! I felt a bit out of my comfort zone. Yet working with Paul, leadership was initially shared, we gathered offers of activities from parents and staff, and arranged a programme and timetable for the Arts Week. Parents offered to teach children to make wooden boxes, flower arrange, line dance, make puppets, sing, and play the banjo. Staff took children to the pantomime in the city's theatre, a circus troop came in and taught children circus

(Continues)

(Continued)

skills such as juggling, and a dance group taught Indian dancing. From the programme of activities, leadership of the Arts Week was shared. I was responsible for the infant department and Paul for the junior department. We led and coordinated the planned activities, resources and staff in our department. Our review meeting at the end of each afternoon helped us to reflect on the day's events and our leadership.

At the end of the week, I'd been pushed out of my comfort zone of the classroom into the wider zone of the primary school. I had gained personal and professional confidence, knowledge, understanding and skills of leadership, and gained an insight into my own leadership pedagogy through leading the Arts Week. I realized the head teacher had given me this leadership opportunity to develop leadership capability. This gave me a taste of leadership and a building block for future leadership roles and responsibility.

The following questions will help you reflect upon your experience of developing leadership capability.

 Questions for reflection

For existing and aspiring leaders

Consider an opportunity you have taken to demonstrate leadership.

- Describe the leadership opportunity.
- *Who* gave it to you?
- *What* did you do?
- *How* did you lead?
- *What* did you learn about leadership?
- *What* did you learn about your own leadership practice and capability?
- Identify an aspect of leadership you did well.
- Identify an aspect of leadership you could improve.

The *Nutbrown Review* (Nutbrown, 2011: 46) of early education and childcare qualifications and *Foundations for Quality* (Nutbrown, 2012), highlighted the notion of inclusive leadership, of every qualified practitioner being able to lead in some capacity, for example, a group, room or setting. Therefore developing leadership capability and capacity within an organization is important for the sustainability of the organization. Distributed, shared and participatory leadership builds leadership capability through empowerment; distributed leadership in educational contexts and integrated practice is now considered.

Distributed leadership

The distributed model of leadership calls for a move away from the traditional vision of leader as one key individual, towards a more collective vision where the potential for leadership rests within various formal and informal leaders; in essence, the maximization of human potential within an organization. This model of leadership has unmistakable ties with concepts such as participative or collaborative leadership (Leithwood and Levin, 2005). There are three distinctive characteristics of distributed leadership identified by Woods et al. (2005: 441–4). The first is linked to concertive action (Gronn, 2002), which recognizes that the pooling of the initiatives and expertise of all available stakeholders, rather than relying on the initiative and expertise of one stakeholder, will produce a product or energy which is greater than the sum of their individual actions. The second distinctive characteristic is the 'openness of boundaries', where the net of potential leaders is widened to recognize all members of the community including parents. Finally, and linked to the latter characteristic, is 'leadership according to expertise'. This refers to the view that expertise is peppered throughout and organization, internally and externally, and in a 'mutually trusting and supportive culture' this expertise can be used to maximize potential.

Leadership should be more participative than directive, more enabling than performing, something advocates of distributive leadership concur with; Harris (2002: 3) defines distributed leadership as 'multiple sources of guidance and direction following the contours of expertise in an organisation, made coherent through a common culture'. This definition acknowledges the very active role the formal leader, for example, the head teacher, setting or centre leader, still holds in creating an atmosphere and environment where authentic distributive leadership can emerge. Successful organizations meld strong 'personalized' leadership at the top with 'distributed' leadership. Muijs et al. (2004), support this view of distributed leadership. They concluded that 'while early years practitioners are committed to heightening professionalism, the most appropriate means of realising this is not through entrepreneurial approaches but rather through collaborative, cooperative and community oriented lines' (ibid., 166–7).

Discussing the Ofsted (2003b) report regarding leadership and management, David Bell argued towards this vision of distributive leadership, stating:

> It is no longer true that leadership and management are the sole responsibility of the head teacher ... high-quality leadership and management must now be developed throughout a school's organization if they are to meet the new challenges facing them in the drive to raise standards and promote social inclusion in all our schools.

This task of developing an atmosphere conducive to authentic distributive leadership is not easy, especially considering the dichotomies that exist between the criteria of distributive leadership and the current system of educational accountability. Jackson (2003: xiv), in considering building leadership capacity for school improvement, addresses the complications involved in adopting the model of distributed leadership, highlighting the biggest challenge as that of reshaping the current 'concept of school as an organisation' towards an organism, that is, ever changing. He goes on to argue that the only way of achieving this restructured version of school, is via successful distributed leadership; therefore presenting a paradox.

Transformational leadership influences the collaboration of teachers. Woods et al. (2005) highlight the importance of context in determining the possibility for distributive leadership to emerge; some will create and sustain conditions within which it can flourish, while others, hierarchical or directive in nature, thwart this emergence. Wallace (2001), in highlighting the risks of distributive leadership, identifies the deterrence preventing heads or setting leaders from relinquishing control. Head teachers are confronted by a heightened dilemma; their greater dependence on colleagues disposes them towards sharing leadership. In a climate of unprecedented accountability, however, they may be inhibited from sharing because leadership should empower colleagues to confidently act in leaderful ways. The head teacher in delegating leadership and responsibility in distributed leadership also has to take an overview and monitor outcomes. Hatcher (2005: 256) raises the question about the feasibility of authentic distributive leadership and democracy in the school setting when he asks, 'where does strategic power ultimately lie, with the head teacher, or with all those directly involved in the school?' According to government mandates and external expectations, the ultimate responsibility lies with the leader. Hatcher goes on to argue that participatory approaches that operate within a head teacher-dominated hierarchy of power can provide a much more congenial school regime; participation is nominally inclusive, authority is exclusive.

Distributed leadership in integrated practice

The concept of leadership belonging to everyone and leadership being distributed and shared in a collective leadership team is central to leading multi-disciplinary teams in integrated practice. The collective team undertakes differing leadership roles, actions and functions under the deliberate action of a designated leader who delegates leadership tasks and responsibilities (Jones and Pound, 2008). This is evident in integrated practice in which health, education and social service professionals work together in a multi-agency team.

The delivery of integrated practice within children's centres and children's services requires the development of ways to working for better health, social and educational outcomes for children. This involves a culture change for staff used to working within narrower and professional services-based boundaries of health, social and educational services (Siraj-Blatchford et al., 2007). The emerging range of leadership roles, such as family support team leader, intervention coordinator, parent advisory team leader and extended schools service coordinator, requires change in how leadership is viewed (Duffy and Marshall, 2007) from a single leader to leadership of specialist teams, each specialist team with a leaderful team of specialists. The leadership of diverse multi-disciplinary teams has challenges and opportunities to ensure children and families benefit from complementary specialisms and joint working (Siraj-Blatchford et al., 2007).

Leading diverse partnerships is one of the national standards in 'Draft national standards for leadership of SureStart children's centre services' (Siraj-Blatchford and Hallet, 2012). Leaders in children's centres and children's services have responsibility for leading integrated practice through leading diverse partnerships in multi-professional working. Leading diverse partnerships involves promoting and leading a culture which reflects and respects the diversity of the local community and agencies within children's centre services and across children's services, and the ability to develop, inspire and motivate multi-disciplinary teams, so that their individual and collective strengths are deployed effectively and professional expertise respected. Such leaders foster a climate of mutual trust and respect that facilitates effective partnership, communication, collaboration and integrated working practices, and encourage, mobilize, connect and support multi-agency practitioners to work together to make a collective difference to the lives of children and families. Effective team leadership in which leadership is distributed and shared, results in high-quality interaction between team members, a culture of trust and openness, and shared understandings (Rodd, 2013). Integrated practice involves structural, relational and participatory approaches to service delivery. The interplay between these approaches encourages participatory and collaborative leadership (Davis and Smith, 2012). The following questions will help you reflect upon your experience of distributed and shared leadership within educational and integrated contexts.

 Questions for reflection

For existing leaders

Consider a context where you distributed and shared leadership with another or others.

- Describe the leadership context and experience.
- *Why* did you distribute and share leadership?
- *Who* did you share leadership with?
- *Why* did you choose them?

(Continues)

(Continued)

- *How* did you distribute leadership?
- *What* was your role?
- *How* did the experience of sharing leadership make you feel?
- Identify one key learning point about distributed leadership from the experience.

For aspiring leaders

Consider a context in which you shared leadership with another or others.

- Describe the leadership context and experience.
- *Who* did you share leadership with?
- *Who* asked you to share leadership? Or did you volunteer?
- *Why* did you distribute and share leadership?
- *How* did you share leadership?
- *What* was your role?
- *How* did the experience of sharing leadership make you feel?
- Identify one key learning point about distributed leadership from the experience.

 Summary

The chapter discussed the leadership practice of empowering others to lead through influence, cultivating leadership capability within a staff team and developing leadership capacity within an organization. Transformational leadership as a process by which a leader fosters group or organizational performance is explored referring to national and international contexts. Distributed leadership in which leadership is shared among others is discussed through educational and multi-professional contexts. Case studies provide leadership examples of practice; questions for reflection enable existing and aspiring leaders to reflect upon their experience of empowering leadership practice.

→ The next chapter continues discussion about the leadership theme, *empowering leadership* in effective and caring leadership in the early years, examining the leadership practice about the process of change and the leader's role in *leading change* within an early childhood organization.

Further reading

Davis, J.M. and Smith, M. (2012) *Working in Multi-professional Contexts*. London: Sage. Chapter 4 in this book, 'Traditional structures of multi-professional leadership and management', discusses participatory leadership through a case study of an integrated children and family service.

Dumay, X. and Galand, B. (2012) 'The multilevel impact of transformational leadership on teacher commitment: cognitive and motivational pathways', *British Educational Research Journal*, 38(5): 703–30. This research study of French-speaking Belgian schools indicates transformational leadership affects teachers' commitment to their school.

Osgood, J. (2012) *Narratives from the Nursery: Negotiating Professional Identities in Early Childhood*. London: Routledge. This book explores constructions of identity, and the negotiation of power that shapes relationships, agency and reinforces social inequalities.

Woodrow, C. and Busch, G. (2008) 'Repositioning early childhood leadership in action and activism', *European Early Childhood Education Research Journal*, 16(1): 83–93. This article explores some dimensions of leadership activism in early childhood and how it is understood and practised in Australian early childhood contexts.

8

Empowering leadership: the process of change

Chapter overview

The leadership practice of *leading the process of change* within the *empowering leadership* theme in effective and caring leadership in the early years is explored in this chapter. One of the key skills required by those leading settings, schools, centres and services is the ability to understand the process of change, to lead, implement and sustain change which is both internally and externally motivated and mandated. This is especially important given the current context of change in the early years sector which has brought increasing attention and accountability to those in positions of leadership.

This chapter will:

- consider the process of change for organizational improvement
- explore catalytic leadership in leading change
- discuss system leadership in school improvement
- reflect upon leaders' experiences of leading change
- provide opportunity for professional reflection about leading change.

The context for change

Change is all around us and is part of everyday life, involving transition, modification, adaptation and accommodation. Change is part of the evolving early childhood landscape informed by local and community initiatives, national government policy, international agreements such as the 1989

United Nations Convention on the Rights of the Child and the 2002 Barcelona Objectives from the European Union. International conventions and declarations are not the only ways in which early childhood policies in any one country can be influenced. The ideas and pedagogical theories from Froebel, Montessori, Vygotsky and Piaget, and pedagogical practices from Reggio Emilia pre-schools in Northern Italy and the Te Wharika curriculum in New Zealand, can influence change in provision and practice (Baldock et al. 2013).

In the climate of government review and subsequent reform in policy in England from the Allen, Field, Munro, Tickell, Nutbrown reviews (2010–12) and the Truss Report *More Great Childcare* (DfE, 2013), early years leaders, educators and teachers are working in a changing and emerging early years landscape. Early years leaders are in the forefront of leading government policy into provision and practice. Leadership is agency for change and leaders are change-makers (CWDC, 2008). Whalley (2011) argues the overall aim of significant change in the sector has been the move towards increased professionalism and raising the quality of provision for young children and families.

Change heightens uncertainty and increases ambiguity (McCall and Lawlor, 2000). How an individual and an organization react to change impacts upon the effectiveness of change. These two leaders' reflections from the REPEY research study highlight the difficulty some leaders face in reconciling change in curriculum delivery.

 Case study: Leader's reflections – reacting to change

The nursery teacher from nursery class 1 feels that curriculum changes have affected her role in the amount of paperwork she has to manage and also the rate of change: 'You just get your head around one thing then you've got to change it a bit more'. This observation and complaint seems to resonate throughout educational sectors in regard to top-down strategies and expectations from government. However, she does believe that the developments have improved her practice; which is supported by the fact that she takes ownership of the strategies implemented or passed down, rather than attempting to take them on fully and without reflection for her current setting and practice.

The nursery teacher from nursery class 2 reflects upon her attitude to change in government mandates:

> We've always been very careful not to pick up trends as they've gone along and we've tried to change in more subtle ways as we've

(Continues)

(Continued)

gone along rather than swoop from one system to another. Any changes we've undertaken have always been within what we're doing so that they've almost been imperceptible as they've happened. But over time you can see that there's been quite a lot of change ... [for instance] we've made sure that we are aware of what the Curriculum Guidance says and we've spent time matching it to our current practices and we've found that our current practice fits into it quite nicely whatever way you care to look at it.

To lead change it is important to understand the process of change, and the role a leader plays in orchestrating change. The process of change as agency for organizational development in a cycle of review and implementation has three phases, as illustrated in Figure 8.1.

1. Agency for change
2. Review
3. Engagement with change.

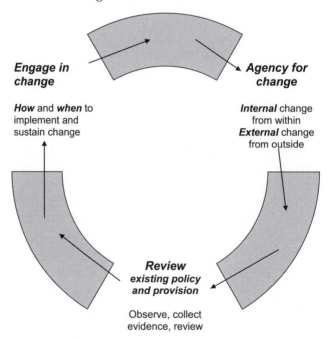

Figure 8.1 The process of change

The process of change

The need or agency for change is identified. A change agent becomes a lever for change. A change agent is a driver for organizational change and begins the change process. This may be an external agent such as government policy, a mandate from the local authority or funding body. The Truss Report (DfE, 2013) is an external lever for change in provision in the early years sector in England, particularly in the development of graduate pedagogical leadership, the focus being on educational outcomes for children and higher staff:child ratios.

The change driver may be an internal agent from within the organization or service, for example, the appointment of a new head teacher promotes change within the school. Rodd (2013) identifies a variety of types of internal change at different levels in early childhood settings: incremental, induced, routine, crisis, innovative and transformational. Induced change emerges from the need to change an aspect of practice relating to people or processes, for example, the reorganization of a key person system in a setting. In innovative change, the leader seeks to introduce new practices to improve provision and practice (Whalley, 2011), for example, setting up a story sack library for children and parents to promote parental involvement in young children's literacy learning.

The next phase in the process of change is a time to review existing policy and provision through observing and collecting evidence. Review questions such as, 'What are we already doing?' 'What works well?' enable reflection, leading to the next phase in the change process, that is, engagement in change. What change can be implemented for improvement in outcomes for children and families or service delivery? The practicalities of how and when to implement change, the process of monitoring and sustaining change can then be considered and planned for.

Leading change

Those responsible for leading change and innovation must ensure that the people they elect to implement the intended changes are provided with intellectual, emotional and practical support. Change that is devoid of consultation and support will, in the long run, inevitably fail. The absence of a sense of ownership and established collective responsibility and purpose amongst the individuals responsible for implementing the changes can lead to dissenting interpretations of the expected change. Promoting a culture of change with the centrality of communication and consultation in the process of change provides a framework for implementing change (Siraj-Blatchford and Manni, 2007).

An effective leader ensures all colleagues are part of the change process, leading collaboratively through professional dialogue underpinned by early childhood knowledge and values (Colloby, 2009). The speed of change can affect implementing and sustaining change. Successful implementation of change is introduced gradually through understanding, ownership and being involved in decisions for implementing change.

Resistance to change occurs when change is introduced quickly. Participants are not informed, therefore they feel threatened and insecure (Jones and Pound, 2008). A leader needs to explain the benefits of change for children, parents, practitioners or the organization as this will help staff feel involved, have understanding and ownership of change (Jones and Pound, 2008) as the leader in the next case study demonstrates.

 Case study: Leader's reflections – engaging with change

Meera, an early years leader in the LLEaP project, is very aware of the time required in leading and engaging with change in her private daycare setting.

> There is constant change within the setting and we all have to adapt our ways of working to respond to government changes and requirements. I also feel patience is vital – change is a slow process if you want it to be effective. You can't climb a mountain in a day and I encourage our team to feel relaxed in their approach to change – it's good to take time and reflect as we go along.

The challenge for early childhood leaders is to lead the process of change in a participatory way, providing opportunities for staff to engage in the process of organizational decision-making (Bush, 2011). Rodd (2013) identifies six aspects in leadership for change. First, a leader has to initiate change with vision and inspiration, followed by careful planning which may be in an action plan of long- and short-term goals. A leader should have decision-making skills and effective communication skills. There will be some resistance to change, therefore a leader should be confident in conflict management and be sensitive in handling people involved in the change or who are affected by the change. In facing significant change, leadership is the art of mobilizing others (Kouzes and Posner, 2007). Leaders therefore must be skilled in change management processes if they are to act successfully as agents of change and motivate others to follow (Van Knippenberg and Hogg, 2003). The attitude to change a leader adopts influences how others view the change process and how change is led and managed. Kavanagh and Ashkanasy (2006) suggest that members of an organization want transparency in change processes, where leaders explain the reasons for change so all involved are knowledgably familiar with the change taking place. Leaders should ensure training and support are given to employees for their questions to be answered, a space for their anxiety and fears to be expressed, where support from peers is available and motivation is maintained. Parry (2011) agrees that during the change process it is important for leaders of the organization to create a safe environment for employees, in which they feel consulted and involved as part of the decision-making process.

Effective leaders are reflective people with a sense of agency who become change-makers within their work contexts and more widely within their professional field (Costley and Armsby, 2007). Through reflective practice, practitioners have the potential to transform what they do and what children and families experience (Paige-Smith and Craft, 2011), and have agency for professional change in pedagogy, provision and professional practice. Leadership styles for change agency are now examined.

Catalytic and system leadership

A graduate early years leader's role (EYP) is to be a change agent to improve and shape practice (CWDC, 2006) as a leader of practice (Whalley, 2011). This role has provoked new ways of envisioning leadership, in which the graduate leader acts as a catalyst for change within their setting, bringing about internal change to create something new (McDowall Clark, 2010). This model of catalytic leadership reconceptualizes early childhood leadership, challenging the view that leadership comes from 'above' or from 'the front', as leadership comes from anywhere within the organization (Reed and Canning, 2012). In McDowall Clark's research (2012) participants began to recognize that leadership does not have to take the form of controlling or directing others' actions, but can be non-directive and influencing. A key factor of this non-directive leadership style is an approach which builds incrementally through small steps rather than dramatic intervention.

The purpose of change is to improve the quality of provision. This notion of change for continuous improvement is included in the 'Draft national standards for leadership of SureStart children's centre services' (Siraj-Blatchford and Hallet, 2012). The national standard 'Leading change and continuous improvement' requires leaders to identify, implement and sustain change to drive children's centre service improvement (Siraj-Blatchford and Hallet, 2012: 16). Long-term quality improvement requires commitment from leaders, practitioners and teachers rather than short-term change resulting from obedient compliance. Reed and Canning, (2012) highlight that a leader with authority by job title can impose change but a catalytic leader brings change through progressive action.

Leadership concerning improvement is purposeful; improvement is change with direction, sustained over time, that moves entire systems, raising the average level of quality and performance while decreasing the variation among units and engaging people in understanding why some actions are better than others (Hopkins, 2005). System leadership can be a catalyst for schools to work together to improve each other in a framework of social justice and moral purpose. Gold et al.'s (2002) research about moral leadership found evidence, in Ofsted-rated 'outstanding' special, primary and secondary schools, that heads demonstrated the following values and beliefs in their leadership style and practices: inclusivity, equal opportunities, equity and justice, high expectations, engagement with stakeholders, cooperation, teamwork, commitment and understanding.

The development of system leaders in autonomous federations or groups of schools enables the sharing of best practice, and capacity to transfer and sustain innovation across groups of schools with system leaders taking greater responsibility for neighbouring schools. A federation head teacher leads more than one school, their time away from one school allowing an associate head or deputy head to lead in their absence, so developing leadership capability. System leadership concerns networking, collaboration and partnership working. In aiming for higher standards and to provide better schools for all children, policy and practice has to focus on system improvement and the use of highly differentiated improvement strategies. This means the school head teacher has to be almost as concerned about the success of other schools as they are about their own school. Sustained improvement of schools is not possible unless the whole system is moving forward (Hopkins, 2005). Emerging systems leadership practices among practitioners in the early years might help to bring about system-wide quality improvements (Siraj-Blatchford and Wah Sum, 2013) for Foundation Stage leaders across the early years sector, including private voluntary providers and children's centres.

Leithwood and Riehl (2003) define the role of system leaders: they *set direction* by creating a vision and being committed to the process of school improvement; *develop people* by leading in learning for staff and children; have the capacity to disseminate and share best practices to address school variation; *develop the organization* by developing effective systems in behaviour, staffing and curriculum; and build effective relationships to change contexts at all levels. System leaders express their moral purpose through measuring their success in raising pupil achievement and narrowing the gap in educational outcomes. They understand personalized learning to enable individual curriculum access. Their schools are developed as personal and professional learning communities, with relationships built across and beyond each school to provide a range of curriculum and learning experiences and opportunities for continuous professional learning. They strive for equity and inclusion through working on curriculum context and culture. System leaders realize that the classroom, school and system levels all impact on each other. They fundamentally understand that in order to change the larger system you have to engage with it in a meaningful way (Hopkins, 2005).

The chapter has discussed the process of change and some leadership practices in leading change. The following case study is reflective writing by a master's student, Maryan, who teaches in a primary school, about how she led change in teaching phonics within her school.

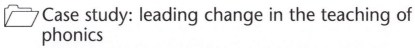 Case study: leading change in the teaching of phonics

The Independent Review of the Teaching of Early Reading (the Rose Report) recommended that systematic phonics should be taught across all schools in England (DCSF, 2006). Systematic phonics is taught using a prescribed scheme that sets out an order in which the children should be taught letters and sounds, children gradually learn more sounds or phonics in a prescribed order (De Graff et al., 2009). There are several different schemes that schools use to teach phonics. The Office for Standards in Education (Ofsted), the inspection agency for schools, endorses a systematic phonics approach, that each school should choose a teaching phonics scheme that is used consistently throughout the school (Ofsted, 2012). As Literacy Coordinator in the primary school for children from 5 to 11 years old, I was tasked by the Senior Leadership Team to lead the implementation of a new phonics scheme across the school. This was to be a significant change for many practitioners in the early years department and across the school as each year group used different schemes and resources to teach phonics, spelling and reading.

The reason for the change in policy was explained to all staff members during a development day 'Preparing for Ofsted's school inspection'. While the decision for change was made by the Senior Leadership Team, the change was seemingly accepted and welcomed by staff members as a necessary and positive initiative. The change was embedded within the school's overall vision to raise children's educational achievement, articulated in the School Improvement Plan (SIP).

The phonics scheme chosen to implement throughout the school was 'Read, Write Inc' and as lead teacher for the reception class my role was to ensure that this scheme was implemented across the four reception classes in the school. This involved modelling teaching and assessment, monitoring peers, monitoring transition from the Reception classes which used the early years curriculum (EYFS) to key stage one which used the primary curriculum (National Curriculum) and working closely with the two phase co-ordinators in the school.

The phonics co-ordinator, two phase co-ordinators for the early years and key stage one and myself attended a training day about the phonics scheme. We would feedback our knowledge about the phonics scheme gained from the training to the rest of the teaching staff at the next weekly phase meetings. I attended the phase meetings and handed out the resources and explained their use to all teachers. The next step was to practise teaching using the new phonics scheme; I did this for a week and then modelled lessons for teachers in both phases. Most teachers saw one of my phonics lessons and used this

(Continues)

(Continued)

as a training tool to implement the new scheme into their practice. I then had weekly meetings with teachers to answer any questions or problems that had arisen during their teaching. After half a term of teaching this new scheme, I and the phonics co-ordinator undertook joint observations across the early years and key stage one classes. All teachers were monitored and joint feedback was given. As a result further coaching for some teachers was identified. This involved systematically planning phonics lessons, using the scheme and the resources as well as further observations of exemplary phonics lessons. After observations, time for dialogue was then assigned in order to identify what made the lessons effective or consider what could have been done to further the learning for the children. Differentiation was identified as a particular area that some teachers found difficult to implement due to the structure and pace of the scheme.

As well as the teachers learning and implementing the new phonics scheme, I also thought it necessary to explain the change to parents. I led a parents' meeting after school and explained how the new scheme would affect the structure of phonics teaching for their children. Parents had also previously requested information about the term synthetic phonics so the meaning and approach to teaching of phonics was explained in workshop.

The introduction of this change in the teaching of phonics proved to be a spiral process of action through implementation, review and planning. In my role as lead teacher in the reception class, I regularly monitor the introduction of systematic phonics and the effectiveness in the teaching of reading through observation, talking to staff and parents and looking at the children's achievement.

Maryan in the case study above reflects upon the process of change. Using the illustration of the process of change in Figure 8.1, the following questions will help you reflect upon leading change.

 Questions for reflection

For existing leaders

Consider a change you have led, what was your role in leading, managing and sustaining change?

Agency for change.

- What was the agency for change? Did the need for change come from within, or outside the organization?

Review.

- How did you review existing provision and identify what needed to change?
- How did you observe, and collect evidence? How did this inform your review and plan for change?

Engage with change.

- Who did you identify to lead change? Why did you choose them?
- When and how did you plan to implement change?
- How do you maintain and sustain the change implemented?

Final reflection, what have you learnt about leading change?

For aspiring leaders

Consider the implementation of change you have been involved in, what was your role?

Agency for change.

- What was the agency for change? Did the need for change come from within, or outside the organization?

Review.

- Were you involved in reviewing existing provision and identifying what needed to change?
- If so, how did you observe, and collect evidence? How did this inform the review and plan for change?

Engage with change.

- Were you involved in leading any aspect of change?
- If so, how did you implement change?
- How do you maintain and sustain the change implemented?

Final reflection, what have you learnt about leading change?

Summary

The chapter discussed the leadership practice of leading change within the *empowering leadership* theme in effective and caring leadership in the early years. The process of change for organizational improvement was explored through a discussion of change agency, catalytic leadership and system leadership. Case studies illustrate examples of leaders engaging in change and leading the process of change. Questions for reflection enable existing and aspiring leaders to reflect upon their involvement and leadership of change.

The next chapter defines the fourth leadership theme, *pedagogical leadership*, in effective and caring leadership practices in the early years, examining the leadership practice of *leading learning* in a learning community of practice.

Further reading

Cottle, M. and Alexander, E. (2012) 'Quality in early years settings: government, research and practitioners' perspectives', *British Educational Research Journal*, 38(4): 635–54.

The journal article describes a research study in the UK, the Understanding Quality project, which investigated practitioners' understanding of 'quality' and 'success', and considers the implications of this understanding for services for young children and families.

Jones, C. and Pound, L. (2008) *Leadership and Management in the Early Years.* Maidenhead: Open University Press.

The importance of a leader sharing information, skills and developing positive working relationships is discussed in Chapter 8, 'Leadership in a multi-agency context'.

McDowall Clark, R. (2012) '"I've never thought of myself as a leader but ...": the early years professional and catalytic leadership', *European Early Childhood Education Research Journal*, 20(3): 391–401.

The concept of catalytic leadership whereby graduate early years leaders inspire change rather than lead change through power is discussed in this journal article.

Reed, M. and Canning, N. (2012) *Implementing Quality Improvement and Change in the Early Years.* London: Sage.

The notion of leading change for improving quality in provision and practice is threaded throughout the chapters in this book.

Pedagogical leadership: leading learning

Chapter overview

The theme *pedagogical leadership* in effective and caring leadership in the early years is defined in this chapter. The leadership practice of *leading learning* in its broadest sense is explored. Situating learning at the centre of an organization, developing learning communities of practice and the development of graduate pedagogical leadership are explored.

This chapter will:

- define pedagogy and pedagogical leadership
- examine pedagogical leadership and its contribution to quality of provision, pedagogy and practice
- discuss learning communities of practice
- discuss the development and role of graduate pedagogical leaders
- reflect upon pedagogical leadership practices.

Pedagogy

Pedagogy is an approach to learning and teaching and takes into account the *how* of learning, for example, indoor and outdoor learning contexts, resources, the interactions between children and staff (Siraj-Blatchford and Hallet, 2012). In England, the term pedagogy is used for educational contexts, to describe approaches to teaching in the classroom, group setting or formal education (Petrie et al., 2012). Pedagogy articulates the complexity of teaching, highlighting the need for teachers to make well-informed choices about strategies they use for the interface between the learner and the curriculum (Baumfield, 2013). Baumfield highlights the difference between teaching and pedagogy; teaching describes the actions taken whilst pedagogy also focuses upon the actions taken and on the ideas and values of education that influence the teaching actions. Pedagogy is both the art and the science of knowing how to carry out intentional instruction and purposeful intervention to influence the development of the learner. The best early childhood educators use their knowledge of the interests and capabilities of the children in their care, and a wide range of cultural and intellectual resources to provide children with the most effective and stimulating active learning experiences in their daily work with children (Siraj-Blatchford, 2009).

The term pedagogy is now beginning to be more commonly used within educational contexts and children's learning in the UK. It is frequently used in Europe, however, in Europe the word 'pedagogy' refers to a much broader range of services, covering childcare, early years, youth work, parenting and family support services, and services for young offenders, residential care and play work. Pedagogy relates to a holistic approach to supporting children's overall development. 'In pedagogy care and education meet, to put it another way, pedagogy is about bringing up children; it is "education" in the broadest sense of the word' (Petrie et al., 2012: 225). Pedagogy is a concept that underpins a distinctive approach to practice, service provision, training and national policy. The construct of the child is the foundation of pedagogy; in Europe the child is seen as a social being, connected to others, and with their own distinctive experiences and knowledge. For example, in Sweden, educational policy concerns the development of the whole child, rather than the child defined by narrow cognitive terms (Petrie et al., 2012) such as 'learning outcomes' and 'early learning goals' as used in the English construct of the child. Similarly, practitioners in Europe who work with children are called 'pedagogues' reflecting their holistic approach to working with children and families. For example, pedagogues work with children and parents in pre-schools in the northern region of Reggio Emilia in Italy.

There was an opportunity for England to adopt this model of social pedagogy in 2000–2002 when the nationally recognized professional status 'Early Years Professional' was introduced. The title 'early years pedagogue' was offered to the workforce but after consultation was rejected and Early Years Professional used. In the adoption of this term, there would have been a fundamental change in approach to working with children. However, the introduction of the Every Child Matters (ECM) agenda (DfES, 2004b) lent itself to a holistic, integrated approach to working with children and families from birth to 19 years of age through universal services. The ECM agenda was a policy shift, promoting more information sharing, multi-agency working and an integrated holistic approach to service delivery for children and families by practitioners (Baldock et al.,

2013). The Coalition government in 2010 instigated review of government policy in England. The change of the government department's name from the Department of Children, Schools and Families (DCSF) to the Department for Education (DfE) reflects the government's emphasis from a holistic approach to working with children and families to a cognitive focus on education, educational achievement and schooling. The Truss Report, *More Quality Childcare*, (DfE, 2013) reflects this change in policy; introducing the terms 'early years educator' and 'Early Years Teacher' reflecting their pedagogical leadership roles within the early years context in England. The concept of pedagogical leadership and its influence on quality of provision is now discussed.

Pedagogical leadership

There is a growing consensus that the most important role the leader plays is the promotion of the improvement of teaching and learning. Sammons et al. (1999), among others concerned with identifying what makes a school effective, have confirmed that leaders play a critical role in supporting staff to remain motivated in their pursuit of improving teaching and learning. Evidence from the school improvement literature consistently highlights that effective leaders exercise an indirect but powerful influence on the school's capability to improve upon the achievement of pupils, 'the contribution of leadership to improving organizational performance and raising achievement remains unequivocal' (Muijs et al., 2004: 157). The Ofsted report (2003b) about leadership and management in schools identifies a number of characteristics of high-quality leadership in schools (p. 7):

- There is a clear vision, with a sense of purpose and high aspirations for the school, combined with a relentless focus on pupils' achievement.

- Strategic planning reflects and promotes the school's ambitions and goals.

- Leaders inspire, motive and influence staff and pupils.

- Leaders create effective teams.

- There is knowledgeable and innovative leadership of teaching and the curriculum.

- Leaders are committed to running equitable and inclusive schools, in which each individual matters.

- Leaders provide good role models to other staff and pupils.

The way in which these leadership characteristics are applied in different educational contexts is fundamental to the effectiveness of the leadership. Understanding about how leaders lead learning is developing. Some theories include that it is learning from others such as exemplary teachers, or through accessing and providing ongoing training and support (NCSL, 2004). Three characteristics about high-quality leadership in schools from the Ofsted (2003b) report support this view: leaders inspire, motivate and influence staff and pupils; leaders provide good role models to other staff and pupils; and there is knowledgeable and innovative leadership of teaching and the curriculum.

Leadership was found to be a key element in the quality of early childhood programmes in Australia (Hayden, 1997). Similarly, Muijs et al (2004) in their review of research on leadership in early childhood found in an evaluation of the 'Head Start' programme for young children and families in the USA that competent and stable leadership was a powerful influence on the effectiveness of the programme. Leadership that was committed, competent and respected was one of the main distinguishing factors between the most and least successful programmes. The least successful Head Start programmes were characterized by less experienced leadership, and leaders were less skilful at training and supervising staff, less good at working with schools and the community, and less involved and committed.

The US Head Start programme influenced the development of SureStart children's centres in England, a community-based provision bringing together services especially for children from birth to 5 years and their families in multi-professional ways. The SureStart children's centres offer children and families services that integrate health, childcare, education, enable parental involvement, family support, and provide intervention programmes. Children's centres that provide effective integrated services are improving outcomes for children (Siraj-Blatchford and Hallet, 2012: 14).

Pedagogy, provision and practice in the early years is community focused. Kagan and Hallmark (2001) suggest that leadership in Early Childhood Education has community aspects:

- *Community leadership* connects Early Childhood Education to the community through informing and constructing links among families, services and resources in the community.

- *Pedagogical leadership* forms a bridge between research and practice through disseminating new information and shaping agendas.

- *Administrative leadership* includes financial and personal management.

- *Advocacy leadership* creates a long-term vision of the future of Early Childhood Education. This involves developing a good knowledge and understanding of the field and being a skilled communicator.

- *Conceptual leadership* conceptualizes early childhood leadership within a broader framework of social movements and change.

Pedagogical leadership as a bridge between research and practice is a specific leadership practice at the centre of schools, settings and centres. Traditionally, there has been more emphasis and understanding of pedagogy, educational and curriculum leadership within the school context rather than in integrated service provision in children's centres. The Early Years Foundation Stage curriculum is delivered for all children from birth to 5 years of age in schools, early years settings and children's centres, therefore pedagogical leadership is heightened in the standard 'Lead teaching, learning and development' in the revised 'Draft national standards for leadership of SureStart children's centre services' (Siraj-Blatchford and Hallet, 2012: 14). In this standard, children's centre leaders have responsibility for leading the quality of teaching learning for improving children's development and educational outcomes. In leadership for learning, leaders develop a culture in which learning is at the centre of the organization that encourages and inspires children, practitioners, parents and carers to become enthusiastic, inquiring, independent and successful lifelong learners.

Learning communities of practice

Pedagogical leadership or leadership for learning is a learning-centred approach to leadership. This approach to leadership is activated with a concern or even passion for learning, different from instructional leadership which seems to imply a transmission of knowledge rather than construction, co-construction or creation of knowledge. Leadership for learning concerns the process of learning, with and without instruction, and identifies learners not only as children in the school, setting, centre or service but organization wide, including staff, parents and carers, community members and stakeholders such as governors (MacBeath, 2003). The term 'lead learners' is commonly used for head teachers and setting or centre leaders who establish a learning organization, where learning is at the centre of the organization and there is a desire to discuss the learning process and children's learning progress through reflective dialogue and to access organizational and individual continuing professional learning opportunities, developing as 'learning professionals' (Guile and Lucas, 1999).

The concept of 'pedagogic leadership', in which the leader's role is developing 'human capital' by helping schools become caring, focused and inquiring communities in which teachers work together as members of a 'community of practice', is described by MacNeill et al. (2004: 37–9). He goes on to argue that schools develop intellectual capital by becoming inquiring communities. Intellectual capital is the sum of what everyone in the school knows and shares, which can help the school be more effective in enhancing the learning and development of children. As the amount of intellectual capital increases, the school's capacity to add value to the lives of children increases. The focus on professional issues, pedagogy, provision and practice allows for roles, teaching and leadership practices to develop (Anning and Edwards, 2003), often in communities of practice where members meet to share a concern or passion for something they do and learn how to do it better (Wenger, 1998). Whalley (2005) describes staff's involvement in a community of practice at Pen Green Centre for under 5s and their families, who, as a result of their involvement with higher and further education and the in-service training programme offered which is based at the centre, have taken on small-scale action research projects which address their own questions and concerns. The beneficial effect of the involvement in research and further education is the addiction to inquiry; staff appear propelled into a cycle of inquiry. In this instance, involvement is not passive. It is not simply being involved in others' research and in answering other people's questions. Instead, it is involvement which promotes the active consultation and participation of staff, children and/or other stakeholders, where contextually relevant and pressing concerns and questions drive the research.

Educators' and teachers' involvement in communities of practice helps to develop pedagogical understanding. The following case study demonstrates a graduate early years leader's pedagogical leadership. As she introduces Sustained Shared Thinking pedagogy in a community of practice within her nursery setting, staff are learning and understanding together.

◻⟋ Case study: Leaders' reflections – staff learning together

Martha is a graduate early years leader in a privately owned nursery. She reflects upon her pedagogical leadership.

In our nursery, we have child-centred practice, we follow the children as they lead their own investigations and we sustain their thinking through reflected questioning. Sustained Shared Thinking (SST) is effective interactions between children and adults to support the development of young children's skills, knowledge and attitudes. Sustained Shared Thinking episodes are when two or more individuals work together in an intellectual way to solve a problem, clarify a concept, evaluate activities or extend narratives. During periods of SST both parties contribute to the thinking, develop and extended the discourse. Associated with SST is the adult's skilled use of open-ended questioning, questions that have more than one answer such as, 'what do you do?', 'what would you do?' (Siraj-Blatchford, 2009: 154).

Sustained Shared Thinking was an area from my early years graduate training course that struck a cord with me and was an area that as a staff we really concentrated on developing in our nursery to help children become reflective learners. We video-recorded sustained shared thinking interactions that were taking place in the nursery. At our Development Day 'Reflective educators – reflective children', I showed the previously recorded SST episodes and asked the staff to reflect upon their interactions; how had their questioning enabled the children to be reflective and develop as reflective learners? We shared our ideas and views. From these I developed an action plan about how we can develop SST to enable children to become reflective learners in our nursery.

The case study shows the impact of graduate leadership training and how Martha, as a pedagogical leader, influences and shares knowledge and understanding of SST with others. The development of pedagogical leadership within the early years workforce is further discussed next.

Developing graduate pedagogical leadership

In recent years there has been significant financial investment by the government in England in developing pedagogical leaders through the nationally recognized higher education award, Early Years Professional Status. Graduates with this award are Early Years Professionals (EYP). Early Years Professionals have a leadership of practice role demonstrating and modelling the highest possible commitment to quality early years practice and to lead and improve practice of others across the Early Years Foundation Stage curriculum. The model of EYP leadership of practice fits across all types of settings in the private voluntary and independent sector, a home-based childminder, a voluntary pre-school in a village hall, private nursery or a large children's centre (Whalley, 2011).

Leaders' experience and education level have been related to setting quality in a number of research studies (Muijs et al., 2004). Evidence from the EPPE project identified there was higher quality of provision in settings that integrated care and education and were led by a qualified teacher who supervised less qualified staff (Sylva et al., 2004). In settings where children made better all-round progress, there was strong leadership, a good proportion of staff were graduate qualified, thus making a clear connection between highly qualified staff and high-quality service for children and families. In setting out a vision for early education and childcare, the Truss Report (DfE, 2013: 13) highlights that 'high quality early education and childcare, delivered with love and care, can have a powerful impact on young children'. Therefore the qualifications of staff have significant importance in the quality of provision.

In introducing the EYP as a graduate leader of practice, no nationally specified job description for the EYP role was given (CWDC, 2006). However, a pedagogical leadership role has emerged. The research study Leadership of Learning in Early Years Practice project (the LLEaP project) (Hallet and Roberts-Holmes, 2010) found Early Years Professionals have a defined role as *leaders of learning*; leading learning in pedagogy and practice for children, parents and other practitioners. Their role is comparable to an Early Years Teacher's role.

The EYPS award aimed to develop a cohesive graduate-led workforce within the EYFS curriculum; however, inequality of qualifications of those delivering the curriculum has arisen. In schools, the curriculum is being led by teachers with recognized Qualified Teacher Status (QTS); in early years settings, the same curriculum is led by EYPs with a professional status only. Denied the status of a qualification, the EYP has been positioned almost in opposition to the existing qualifications and status of teachers (Lloyd and Hallet, 2010), producing a qualification gulf in the workforce between the maintained and non-maintained sectors. The qualifications required for working with young children and models of professional practice are culturally specific to a country, formed by government policy. In New Zealand, young children are taught by teachers. In many European countries young children are taught by pedagogues. The European model of a pedagogue or an increase of teachers was not selected by the Labour government in England in the development of a graduate workforce (Oberheumer, 2005). A new model of an Early Years Professional, with a different training to that of a qualified teacher, was designed, with a role as a leader of practice, rather than a teaching role.

Garrick and Morgan's (2009) research of the impact of the role of teachers working in children's centres identified that teachers brought vital profess-ional knowledge and experience, and were successful in developing practice and staff confidence through a range of leadership styles. The Nut-brown Review (DfE, 2012: 46) highlighted the importance of pedagogical leadership in qualified practitioners' roles; leading practice within a room, leading practice across a number of rooms, leading practice across a setting, providing overall pedagogical leadership for a setting, working directly with children and families, and supporting staff with lower qualifications. The Truss Report (DfE, 2013) furthers graduate pedagogical leadership in early years settings by introducing Early Years Teachers to lead further improvements in quality provision. The EYP's pedagogical leadership role is recognized in the Truss Report (DfE, 2013: 44) 'existing Early Years Professionals will in future be seen as equivalent to Early Years Teachers (EYT) and therefore not need to obtain QTS to increase their status'. The role of EYTs as specialists in early childhood development and trained to work with babies from birth to 5 years of age. The training route and new teachers' standards will build upon the strengths of the EYPS programme. These recommendations should bridge the qualifications divide between the maintained and non-maintained schools and settings in England, and reflect international pedagogical leadership practices and teaching roles.

In the next case study, from the LLEaP project, two graduate leaders with EYPS working in different early years settings reflect upon their pedagogical leadership role as leaders of learning.

 ## Case study: Leaders' reflections – a leader of learning

Amelia's reflections

A leader of learning – this is a challenging concept, where does the leading begin in my setting? Who am I? How have I become a leader and what skills have I used or do I use?

I would like to think I lead the learning from the nursery floor! By this I mean that I lead children's learning from their level. I spend a lot of time with the children (unfortunately not enough time) but I would say that I am with the children ninety to ninety-five percent of the session. Observing the children within their play has enabled me to develop their learning to take them onto the next steps or to reinforce their play and activities. However the ability to extend their learning in this way has not just been due to my interaction with them, it is scaffolded by philosophy and vision of the staff. Staff believe that children are in charge of their learning and work hard to support this on a daily basis, planning resources, activities, space to accommodate their needs. Leading learning – perhaps I would like to change this to, following the learning with children, our child-centred pedagogy puts the child at the centre of the learning process, we support and extend their learning in an individual way.

Leading learning with the staff has developed over the years I have owned the nursery, built on previous experience as a class teacher – looking at how I do this is complex. I try to be democratic and include everyone's ideas and beliefs as well as possible. I am happy to accommodate the ideas of staff and positively encourage them to take responsibility for different areas. I try to play to their 'strengths' and support their 'weaknesses' and I am aware that the staff do the same for me. I try to treat everyone fairly, but differently as appropriate and try to acknowledge all the extra work they do.

What leadership skills do I need to lead learning? I have vision, imagination and empathy in abundance; vision for leading children, parents, staff and the nursery school towards a creative and child-centred education and for leading innovations. Imagination in order to cope with changes, how to implement the above. Empathy to imagine how children, parents, staff and nursery school will respond to initiatives and ideas. To work out the best approaches to problems, ideas and innovation to provide a nursery school with learning at the centre for children.

(Continues)

(Continued)

Myria's reflections

My role as an early years leader in respect to leading learning has been to collaborate with those I work with to reflect upon their beliefs, practice and provision to enable change. I have focused on the image of the strong and powerful child in my pedagogy, because ultimately, the child is at the centre of all that we do. Children and their childhoods are important. I hope to inspire others and support them to be co-constructors with children and families, using language, active learning, critical and creative Sustained Shared Thinking, but also respect, care and love to construct meaningful and significance learning.

The following questions will help you to consider your own pedagogy and how this has influenced your pedagogical leadership.

 Questions for reflection

For existing leaders

- Write a paragraph to describe your pedagogy.
- Identify any key aspects of your pedagogy that is evident in your pedagogical leadership and how you lead learning.
- Give an example of your effective pedagogical leadership. How do you know your leadership of learning was effective? What evidence do you have? How can you sustain and maintain the outcome of your effective pedagogical leadership?

For aspiring leaders

- Write a paragraph to describe your pedagogy.
- Describe an example of how you have led learning with children, parents or staff. How do you know it was effective?
- Describe an experience of pedagogical leadership. Did the pedagogical leader influence your own pedagogy, provision and practice? If so, how did this happen?

Final reflection – what have you learnt about leading learning and the pedagogical leader's role?

Summary

The chapter discussed the leadership practice of leading learning within the *pedagogical leadership* theme in effective and caring leadership in the early years. Pedagogy and pedagogical leadership are defined. The pedagogical leadership practice of *leading learning* in its broadest sense is explored; situating learning at the centre of an organization, developing a learning culture and community of practice for staff, children, parents and the wider community is explored. The contribution of graduate early years pedagogical leadership to the quality of provision and practice is discussed. The development of graduate pedagogical leadership for leading learning across all settings and schools and a discussion about the role of the Early Years Teacher in light of the Truss Report (DfE, 2013) is given. Two graduate leaders reflect upon their role of leading learning in their early years settings. Some reflective questions give opportunity for existing and aspiring leaders to consider pedagogical leadership practices.

→ The next chapter continues discussion about the fourth leadership theme, *pedagogical leadership* in effective and caring leadership in the early years, examining the leadership practice of *reflective learning*, considering the leader's role in supporting staff's pedagogical leadership through continuing professional learning and development.

Further reading

Beckley, P. (2012) 'Pedagogy in practice', in P. Beckley (ed.), *Learning in Early Childhood*. London: Sage. pp. 43–60.
  This chapter provides information about key thinkers in early years provision and their influence upon pedagogy and practice. The chapter also provides a discussion about pedagogy in Scandinavia, particularly Norway.
Garrick, R. and Morgan, A. (2009) 'The children's centre teacher role: developing practice in the private, voluntary and independent sector', *Early Years: An International Journal of Research and Development*, 29(1): 69–81.
  This paper disseminates research about the impact of the role of the teacher in two children's centres in England and identifies some of the supporting and limiting factors that influence outcomes. Implications for policy and practice are discussed.
Pardhan, A. (2012) 'Pakistani teachers' perceptions of kindergarten children's learning : an exploration of understanding and practice', *Frontiers of Education in China*, 7(1): 33–64.
  This journal article considers perceptions of children's learning and classroom practice to support learning in the Pakistani early years educational context.
Petrie, P., Boddy, J., Cameron, C., Heptinstall, E., McQuail, S., Wigfall, S. and Wigfall,

V. (2012) 'Pedagogy: a holistic, personal approach to work with children and young people across services', in L. Miller, R. Drury and C. Cable (eds), *Extending Professional Practice in the Early Years*. London: Sage. pp. 221–38.

Chapter 18 discusses research carried out at the Thomas Coram Research Unit in London about social pedagogy, a distinctive way of working with children and policy development in Europe.

Siraj-Blatchford, I. (2009) 'Early childhood education (ECE)', in T. Maynard and N. Thomas (eds), *An Introduction to Early Childhood Studies*. 2nd edn. London: Sage. pp. 148–60.

The chapter provides a comprehensive overview of pedagogy and curriculum within Early Childhood Education (ECE); including an emergent curriculum; play and Early Childhood Education; effective pedagogy and Sustained Shared Thinking; international ECE models; and other common pedagogical models of ECE.

10

Pedagogical leadership: leading reflective learning

Chapter overview

The leadership practice of *leading reflective learning* within the *pedagogical leadership* theme in effective and caring leadership in the early years is explored in this chapter. The chapter discusses the generally accepted view of the importance of promoting staff's continuing professional learning and development through reflective practice and collaborative dialogue.

This chapter will:

- discuss the importance of continuing professional learning and development for quality of provision
- explore how pedagogical leaders can provide opportunities for reflective dialogue and learning
- examine approaches to monitoring practice
- consider approaches to giving feedback and signposting for further development of practice
- reflect upon leaders' approaches to leading reflective learning.

Continuing professional learning and development

There is a general expectation for teachers and educators to be committed to continue their professional learning throughout their career to develop as a professional. Continuing Professional Development

(CPD) activity includes professional training, emphasizing practical information, professional education emphasizing theory, and research-based knowledge and professional support to develop job experience and performance. These are carried out individually or with others, enabling practitioners, educators and teachers to think about their practice, improve ways of working for the benefit of children's learning and development, and enhance their knowledge and skills, their personal and professional growth, self-confidence and job satisfaction (Bubb and Earley, 2007). There are a range of CPD events; training days, conferences, in-service courses, school-based projects, short- and long-term courses in higher education, staff development days and meetings, network meetings, coaching, mentoring sessions, visiting other schools and settings to see provision and practice. The Teaching Development Agency (TDA, 2008) identified the value of reflective activity within the process of professional learning for developing an individual's professional attributes, knowledge, understanding and skills. Opportunities for reflection support individual's professional needs to improve their practice.

The REPEY study found in analysis of the responses given by interviewees (leaders, managers and early years staff), and the exploration of policy and other documentation regarding approaches to professional development, a verbal and written commitment and conviction to the importance of ongoing professional development. However, upon further analysis of these data, it is clear that a great deal of the professional development opportunities experienced by those in leadership, management and staff positions tends to be, as Rodd (2013) describes, general in-service or short courses. In a minority of cases, there was evidence that the leader, manager or another member of staff was pursuing more long-term courses, for example, a diploma course in management studies, and degree courses in early years education. In some instances, respondents refer back to their original training courses when asked either about their involvement in professional development or the training they are relying on to support them in their current work. Some respondents expressed dissatisfaction with the courses they attended, finding them lacking in relevance, follow-up or depth. One manager of a private day nursery response highlights several of these limitations:

> I didn't feel it was in-depth enough, and it would have been beneficial to come back after we had begun to put it into practice, to have some more training, to ascertain if we were doing things 'right', to get advice, share concerns, see what other people from other settings were doing and experiencing.

This same nursery manager goes on to highlight an interesting limitation of the process of cascading back to staff as a means of professional development. In discussing her attendance at a one-day workshop about the teaching of reading, this manager highlights the opportunity to interact with individuals representing a range of early years backgrounds (private/public, nursery school/class, private day nursery, childminders) as one of the main benefits of the day; the opportunity to engage in reflective dialogue with others who offer a different perspective. She carried on to explain that in delivering back the information from the day's workshop to her staff, she became the 'expert', and the kind of interaction and dialogue that she had experienced in listening to different reactions and input from the diverse participants during the workshop could not be reproduced in the staff room of the private day nursery.

This nursery manager's sentiments about the benefits of participant involvement in training sessions were echoed by the manager from a different private day nursery: 'I'd like lots more in-house training; trainers that would come to us and train us all together as a staff. I would also like more training that is designed specifically for us and our particular context.' This desire, of having group training that is designed specifically for a group of educators in an early years setting, is moving towards authentic learning. Authentic learning is defined as learning that employs real-world problems and allows for the exploration and discussion of problems and issues that are relevant to those involved in the learning. Authentic leadership and dialogue lies at the core of organizational learning. Without dialogue, individuals and groups cannot effectively change ideas or develop shared understanding (Parry, 2011). Leaders influence the learning process at and between the individual, group and organizational levels. Authentic leadership impacts upon the type of dialogue that might take place (Mazutis and Slawinski, 2008). The authentic leader encourages open and honest dialogue among organizational members. Dialogue has conversation at its centre, promotes self-awareness, reflection and reflective practice. Leaders shape an organizational culture that encourages open, honest, balanced, congruent and transparent communication (Mazutis and Slawinski, 2008). Authentic leadership is described as a process 'which results in both greater self-awareness and self-regulated positive behaviours on the part of leaders and associates, fostering positive self-development' (Luthans and Avolio, 2003: 243). Being able to reflect upon practice develops self-awareness for professional learning and development. The value of reflection and reflective learning for leaders is included in national leadership training programmes.

Reflective leadership training programmes

Reflection and the development of practitioner's reflective practice are included in the national standards of the two professional awards for early years leaders in England. In the Early Years Professional Status in standards concerning professional development, undergraduate candidates are asked to reflect on and evaluate the impact of their practice, modify approaches where necessary and take responsibility for identifying and meeting their professional development needs (CWDC, 2006). Reardon (2009: 43) likens achieving the EYPS standards and becoming a graduate early years leader, an Early Years Professional, to a reflective journey; candidates require time to reflect, review, analyse, evaluate and record the range of leadership experiences in their own work setting, other settings and in a network. Bruce (2006) explains that the cycle of informed reflection, self-evaluation and development at the centre of the reflective process requires openness and the capability to step back and examine practice in a critical and honest way, identifying aspects of effective practice and exploring elements of practice that are less successful, and challenge practice to make improvements.

The National Professional Qualification for Integrated Children's Centre Leaders (NPQICL) master's level programme has reflection as a central strand in the andragogy to learning and teaching adults. Participants reflectively learn about leadership theories and practices through collaborative reflective processes in the classroom and in leadership learning groups based in children's centres. Individual reflective learning about the leadership practices of leaders in children's centres is facilitated through mentoring sessions; participants individually reflect upon their leadership practice and development with a mentor. Reflective spaces outside the work setting of a children's centre are provided for participants to think, feel and talk about their leadership of integrated practice and development as a leader. The supportive and facilitative mentoring relationship between the mentor and mentee provides great potential for reflective practice (Ruch, 2003). Similarly, the use of a reflective journal throughout the NPQICL programme was found to be an effective tool for reflecting upon leadership practice and development, as it helped leaders to 'think through what to do next or, to work out how things might be done better' (National College for School Leadership, 2008: 7). Participants identify areas of leadership and integrated practice to research, furthering reflective learning and individual and organizational development. This reflective model of Continuing Professional Development concerning the process of examining and exploring an issue of concern triggered from experience, results in a changed and informed perspective, identifying experience as the basis for reflection. This approach to professional development moves the training provider from being an expert deliverer of knowledge to a facilitator of reflection-on-practice (Tarrant, 2000), supporting Schon's (1983) theory of reflection and the development of a reflective practitioner who is able to reflect on their practice and make modifications to improve professional practice. In this model, reflective practice becomes a meeting place between theory and practice (McMillan, 2009), a space in which leaders can make connections between practice and theory. The following four questions form a framework for critical reflective learning about leadership practice.

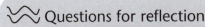 Questions for reflection

For existing and aspiring leaders

What?

- What leadership practices are in my school, setting or centre?
- What leadership theories support these leadership practices?
- What research evidence is there to support the leadership practices in my school, setting or centre?

Why?

- Why are they the preferred leadership practices?
- Why do or don't the leadership practices benefit staff, children and families?

Who?

- Who are the leaders in the school, setting or centre?
- Who are emerging leaders in the school, setting or centre?
- Who are aspiring leaders in the school, setting or centre?

How?

For existing leaders

- How can my reflection about leadership in my school, setting or centre inform and improve leadership practices?
- How can this reflective learning develop new theories or ways of leadership practice?

For aspiring leaders

- How can my reflection about my own leadership practices inform and improve my leadership capability?

Reflection provides a process for leaders and practitioners to implement change in pedagogy, provision and practice. This is discussed within the context of government review, reform and policy.

Reflective learning and practice

There is an emerging importance for early years educators, teachers and leaders to be reflective in the changing landscape of early years provision and practice owing to government review, reform and policy. Reflection provides a process for leaders and practitioners to change the landscape in which they work, with the ability to think about and challenge existing ways of working (Reed, 2008) through reading, dialoguing with others, thinking about theory, research and how these relate to and inform practice. Reflection concerns the reprocessing, reconstruction and understanding of knowledge where the leader and practitioner seeks to make sense of new material, connecting it to what she or he already knows, modifying existing knowledge and meaning to develop and accommodate new ideas (Moon, 1999).

Reflective professional inquiry includes reflective dialogue, conversations about educational issues or problems, involving applying new knowledge, seeking new knowledge, examining teachers' and educators' practice through observation and analysis, joint planning and development to address individual pupils' needs (Stoll, 2013). Action research is a form of self-reflective inquiry, an activity that combines action (practice) and research (reflection) in an individual or collaborative attempt to understand, improve and reform practice (Siraj-Blatchford and Manni, 2007). One of the categories of effective leadership practice in the ELEYS study is encouraging reflection through the development of a community of learners within an early years organization who have a common commitment to reflective, critical practice and professional development. Leaders in effective settings engaged in active involvement in individual and collaborative learning and research, and were both reflective in their own practice and encouraged reflection in their staff.

The development of a learning community of practice consisting of reflective practitioners led by reflective leaders, concerns social learning processes that take place when participants have common interest, share ideas and practices, discuss issues, problem-solve and develop shared understandings and new practices through reflective dialogue (Wenger, 1998). This develops through participation and evolves over time, demonstrating that learning is not static but an emerging process of reflection, improvement and change in professional practice. To develop a learning community of reflective practitioners, the leader establishes a climate of trust, respect and open dialogue, facilitating practitioners to challenge and question practice, theory and research, and to make meaning and develop new theories and ways of working (Hallet, 2013).

Colmer (2008) describes her role in leading such a learning organization and developing Australian early years centres as learning networks. Her work began in one of the centres within the group of early years centres in Australia. The staff working in the child centre in Adelaide were inspired and motivated through devolved leadership and reflectivity. Investment in staff training and development led to extended learning networks and high-quality, integrated provision for children and families. To develop the early years centre as an effective learning network, the centre adopted action learning as a key research methodology. Staff designed and carried out action-learning projects across the children's programmes. A two-year practitioner inquiry project led by nominated staff built upon and furthered their leadership capability. A leadership course for staff at the centre delivered by senior staff included action learning and required staff to collaborate across different groups in the centre. Opportunities for staff to engage in wider professional activity as members of early years reference groups and networks, to attend and present at conferences and undertake secondments, provide professional learning and development and ongoing valuable networking. These activities also recognize staff expertise and establish national networks and connections. Colmer, as a leader, encouraged her staff's reflective professional development. Ways in which leaders can monitor and assess practices and behaviours, and identify areas of strength and areas for professional development, are now considered.

Monitoring practice and promoting reflective professional development

Part of being a community of learners is the recognition and commitment of all towards ongoing development and training. This is linked to the argument that the quality of early years programmes is directly related to the quality of the staff members who work within the settings (Rodd, 2013). The first and most important task educational leaders face is their direct or indirect support and improvement of children's learning and development, their pedagogical leadership focus being on teaching and learning. This is inextricably linked to practitioners in their day-to-day practice and interaction with children, which has a direct effect upon child development. For this reason, it is essential that this practice is monitored and assessed to ensure that the quality of practice provided is at a good standard.

The leaders' commitment to monitoring and assessing the practices and behaviours of early years staff is another way early years leaders can promote the development of a community of learners. Indeed, this process will help in identifying the strengths and limitations of current staff practice and behaviour, and inform the selection of professional development opportunities made available to staff. In most of the early years settings involved in the REPEY study, monitoring and assessment of staff were regarded as important and critical features of the running of the setting. The five examples of nurseries in the next case study show differing aspects of appraisal to promote reflective practice and staff development.

 Case study: Staff development

Sunshine Private Day Nursery

The Sunshine Private Day Nursery provides an excellent example of one centre's commitment to the ongoing assessment and development of staff. This commitment to staff development begins upon entry to the nursery, where all staff members go through an induction programme which focuses on the care and safety of the children. This is followed by an expectation of ongoing training. Ongoing training is provided according to the needs identified through a regular appraisal system that takes place for each individual member of staff every six to 12 months and other regular reviews by senior staff.

(Continues)

(Continued)

The appraisal system itself provides a model whereby the appraiser and appraisee can develop techniques of assessment and identification of training needs.

Members of staff can also choose to attend one or two courses from the programme circulated by the nursery leader from a training company to which the centre is affiliated. Some of the courses on offer include: management, assessment and child protection courses. Other training is provided during regular in-house staff meetings and is conducted by the senior staff themselves. Also, a procedure is in place to ensure that members of staff who attend courses or workshops are given the time and opportunity to report back during staff meetings for the benefit of other staff. The centre manager also subscribes to relevant professional care and educational journals, which are circulated to all staff members, and staff also have access to a library of professional books.

The system of monitoring and appraisal is particularly useful to explore in more depth. The centre manager tries to conduct an appraisal interview with each member of staff every six to 12 months. All staff members are given comprehensive guidelines describing the purpose and procedures of the appraisal system, which appear to show a responsible and mature attitude towards assessing professional performance and linking it directly to ongoing training needs.

Each member of staff is appraised by the centre manager, a senior staff member and one member of staff. This third person represents one of the appraisee's peers, whose presence is aimed to ensure against unfair and biased assessments. Respecting confidentiality is strongly emphasized, and is pertinent to this particular appraisal structure within a fairly small workforce in the setting. All those involved in the process of appraising a member of staff are given training, notes and advice which aim to ensure that appraisals are done fairly and accurately. Appraisers are advised to make objective, professional judgements based on the practices observed and not the individual. The observations and initial assessments are then compared across the three appraisers to ensure that there is a consistency prior to reporting back to the individual monitored and appraised.

There are three parts to the appraisal system. Part one consists of the completion of a pre-appraisal form which is given to each appraisee to complete and submit to their line manager at least a week before the appraisal interview. This form asks for information in relation to matching actual duties with job description, personal assessment relating to performance and any influential factors, training undertaken, perceived future needs, possible targets and possible additional support from management.

Part two involves the appraisal interview. Initially, two members of staff within the appraisee's room (one senior and one peer), put together a staff appraisal which is based on observations of appraisee's performance and interaction with children, her involvement with parents and her level of contribution in the nursery. The line manager, and peer appraiser, then use the appraisal interview to focus on the assessment of general performance, quality of relationships with parents and levels of initiative. Other areas include appearance, ability to relate well to colleagues and children, levels of expertise and maturity, record-keeping skills, and level of interest in professional development. Ratings of between 1 and 4 are given for each area, where 1 is low and 4 is high, and totalled to present a grading. The results form the agenda for discussion between the appraisee and the centre manager. Any identified shortcomings are dealt with first by discussion and followed, if necessary, by a programme of appropriate training within or outside the nursery. Post-appraisal forms are also available for appraisees, giving them an opportunity to write comments or to put forward any questions they have about the assessment. This post-appraisal form offers the individual appraised the opportunity to consider further the issues raised during her discussion with all appraisers and to formulate her own thoughts.

Discovery Nursery School

The staff appraisal system in Discovery Nursery School ensures the regular monitoring by the head teacher of all staff members. The policy clearly states that the purpose of monitoring and evaluation is to improve the quality of teaching and learning, to contribute towards an atmosphere of development and critical collaboration, and to identify and share good practice. The process is ongoing and fairly informal, with the head teacher appraising performance through frequent conversations with staff. However, each member of staff also has a more formal annual meeting, where the head teacher reviews the year and offers each member of staff the individual opportunity to discuss their ideas for continued development and to express any concerns they have. The information gathered during this annual review influences the head teacher's future organizational plans and decisions. In addition to the informal monitoring and conversations and annual review, the head teacher also conducts a programme of observing staff in the room in which they regularly work. Formal observations identify strengths and target areas for development. These targets are confidential, although

(Continues)

(Continued)

if similar ones are identified for several staff members, they are considered for whole staff in-service provision.

The informal–formal model of monitoring and appraisal is one that is described by several managers within our sample of early years settings; though the frequency and procedures differ. Most report that they conduct ongoing, informal observations or discussions in an effort to maintain a grasp on the day-to-day happenings in their settings but then supplement these observations with a more formal approach to identify the strengths and limitations of the staff. All gave constructive feedback and help the staff to use the points to feed forward into their professional practice for development and improvement.

Blue Skies Day Care Centre

A comment made by the manager of Blue Skies Day Care Centre highlights the role feedback can play in promoting more reflective practice. She explains:

> I am always surprised at the insight observers' comments and feedback offer. I think a lot of what we do is intuitive and for better or worse, access to an outside view can be very useful in promoting improved practice or verbalizing existing good practice.

The Giving Tree Nursery School

This is something echoed by the head teacher of The Giving Tree Nursery School who explains that one of the main aims of the process of delivering feedback about practices observed is to ensure that her staff become more reflective in their practice, and enables them to recognize both strengths and limitations. This seems to be taken a step further by the manager of Wind in the Willows Private Day Nursery.

Wind in the Willows Private Day Nursery

In addition to her formal monitoring and assessment procedures, she has also developed a system of peer observation. Here, staff are given non-contact time as an opportunity to observe their colleagues 'at work' with young children as a means of facilitating discussion, increasing reflective practice and assessing how well plans have been realized in practice.

Collaborative reflective dialogue

Reflective practice can be promoted within an early years setting via a routine and consistent system of monitoring and assessment and collaborative dialogue (Siraj-Blatchford and Manni, 2007). Providing opportunity for staff to regularly meet together for reflective dialogue provides a reflective learning culture. This is a common practice in the Italian nurseries in Reggio Emilia region where pedagogues close the nursery and regularly meet to discuss children's learning progression (Abbott and Nutbrown, 2001). In the Discovery Nursery School in the REPEY study, the head teacher closed the nursery school each Wednesday afternoon for staff to participate in collaborative dialogue about children's learning, reflective practice and professional development. The following case study explains how this exposure facilitated reflective dialogue.

 ## Case study: Collaborative reflective dialogue

The head teacher of the Discovery Nursery School reflects:

The early closure of the nursery on Wednesday afternoons is something that we as a staff thought long and hard about, and it is something that is done for a particular reason; it was done because we all felt that we needed time to plan and to explore ways of documenting children's learning – and we actually wanted to give the staff working with the children some quality time to reflect and talk about teaching and learning. The nursery is a very busy place and though staff talk all the time, these conversations tend to be stolen moments ...

These afternoons fulfil a series of purposes, ranging from day-to-day business, to visits from outside consultants, to policy development. In addition to providing a routine time for staff to meet, the Wednesday afternoon closures also ensured that nursery nurses and support staff were able to participate within their working hours. This inclusive environment serves to validate each member of staff and their experiences with the children and parents as unique and invaluable to the ongoing pedagogical discourse. It also supports and promotes a culture of mutual respect, where everyone's input is valued.

Leaders' reflective learning concerns behaviours and attributes mainly with staff, but with parents and children also. These include the ability for a leader to reason, problem-solve, evaluate, give constructive feedback to feed forward into provision and practice, learn from and with others, explain pedagogical beliefs, consider and listen to others' views, consider and observe practices, and explore and challenge theories and research with others (Hallet, 2013). Leaders' ability to give feedback in a constructive and sensitive way and feed forward by signposting ways for colleagues to develop their practice, forms the basis for reflective learning. The following questions provide ways to reflect upon this approach in facilitating reflective learning.

〰️ Questions for reflection

For existing leaders

Consider an example of your leadership practice when you have given some feedback to a member of staff.

- How did you prepare the staff member to receive the feedback?
- When did you give the feedback?
- Where did you give the feedback?
- How did you give the feedback, what did you consider in this process?
- How did you feed forward by signposting ways to develop practice?
- Reflect upon how you fed back and fed forward
  – How did your staff member receive the feedback?
  – How did you feel about the feedback process?
- What have you learnt about your leadership practice of feeding back and feeding forward for reflective learning?
- Is there anything you would do differently another time?

For aspiring leaders

Consider an experience when you received some feedback from a leader.

- How did the leader prepare you to receive the feedback?
- When did you receive the feedback?
- Where did you receive the feedback?
- How did you receive the feedback?
- Did the leader feed forward by signposting ways to develop your practice?
- Reflect upon your experience of receiving feedback and feedforward. Was it a positive or negative experience? Did the leader's interactions help your reflective learning?
- What have you learnt about the leadership practice of giving and receiving feedback?

The chapter has considered ways leaders can promote and support others' reflective learning. However, leaders should demonstrate critical self-reflective leadership, being able to reflect upon personal performance and take account of comments and feedback from others to identify the impact of their leadership practices upon the effectiveness of children's centre services; they should have a personal commitment to continuous professional leadership development, and demonstrate reflective learning for others to aspire to. (Siraj-Blatchford and Hallet, 2012). Leaders in early years settings, schools and centres have responsibility for developing their own leadership practices through critical reflection and self-review within a framework of continuous professional learning and improvement.

Summary

The leadership practice of *leading reflective learning* within the *pedagogical leadership* theme in effective and caring leadership in the early years is explored in this chapter. Ways in which pedagogical leaders provide opportunities for reflective learning through reflective dialogue, promoting opportunities for Continuing Professional Development and approaches to monitoring practice are discussed and illustrated by case studies of leadership practice. The leadership practice of giving feedback for reflective learning is considered. Reflective questions provide opportunity for leaders to consider this particular leadership practice of leading reflective learning.

→ The next chapter 'Leadership stories', is Part 3 and concludes the book. Early years leaders' 'leadership stories' are reflective accounts describing their leadership experiences through illustration and writing; reflecting upon their journeys into leadership, identities as leaders and leadership practices.

Further reading

Bolton, G. (2010) *Reflective Practice: Writing and Professional Development*. 3rd edn. London: Sage.
 This book discusses the value of reflective writing in professional learning and development.
Colmer, K. (2008) 'Leading a learning organisation: Australian early years centres as learning networks', *European Early Childhood Education Research Journal*, 16(1): 107–15.
 This paper describes how a leader established a learning organization and learning networks within early years centres in Australia.
John, K. (2008) 'Sustaining the leaders of children's centres: the role of leadership mentoring', *European Early Childhood Education Research Journal*, 16(1): 53–66.
 The mentoring process for reflecting upon leadership development is discussed in this paper.
Lunenberg, M. and Willemse, M. (2006) 'Research and professional development of teacher educators', *European Journal of Teacher Education*, 29(1): 81–98.

In this journal article a research study in the Netherlands about the professional development of teacher educators found reflection supported their professional development.

Wise, C., Bradshaw, P. and Cartwright, M. (eds) (2013) *Leading Professional Practice in Education*. London: Sage.

A comprehensive book about leading professional practice in education; Part One discusses leading learning and learner leadership and Part Three discusses leading professional development. Chapter 16 by Louise Stoll focuses upon leading professional learning communities.

Part 3

Reflective leadership

Introduction

While teaching students about being reflective and inquiring practitioners, Felicity, an experienced teacher leader in a Montessori school, gave me the following quotation about being reflective which she had found during her reading:

> The creative reflective cycle could be thought of, like a breath, as a vital exchange of energy that goes on between the children and the adults. As breathing is a continuous cycle made up of a progression of stages. The in-breath is the observation; our reading of the environment and what is happening. The pause between in-and-out breath is the revisiting, analyzing and generating of possibilities. The out-breath is our response to the children and the environment of enquiry, our breathing life back into it. This is a continuous cycle that involves a reciprocal exchange between the children and adults.

This quotation by Aguirre Jones and Elders (2009: 12) highlights the importance of reflection being part of our everyday behaviour, seeing and being, as integral to our self as breathing. As practising or aspiring early years leaders we are on a *reflective learning journey* (Hallet, 2013: 125) of professional leadership learning and development. The journey inevitably has twists and turns in the pathways leaders take; through reflective steps the pathway untwists and forms a direction of reflective travel for early years leaders to review, consider and develop their leadership behaviour and practice.

Part 3 is the concluding chapter of the book. Entitled 'Leadership stories' the chapter celebrates women leaders' achievements. The leadership stories are reflective narrative accounts from three early years leaders about their journeys into and through leadership. Their authentic voices are heard through drawing and writing. The stories aim to inspire practising and aspiring leaders to consider their own reflective journeys of discovery, leadership learning and development

11

Leadership stories

Chapter overview

In previous chapters effective and caring leadership practices have been examined and the importance of reflection in leadership practices discussed. In this concluding chapter, these practices are demonstrated through lived experiences of leadership through narrative exploration. Three early years leaders share their autobiographical reflective stories of their journeys into leadership and understandings of their identity as leaders.

This chapter will:

- discuss autobiographical narrative as an approach to understanding professional practice
- consider leadership identity
- share women leaders' stories of their experience of leadership
- provide opportunity for reflective storying of leadership experience.

Reflective storying

The telling of stories is a common practice across all continents and cultures. Narrative is central to human experience and existence, providing opportunity to share the nature and order of events in particular times in history. It helps to define self and personal identity. Autobiographical self-reflection is one of the most important forms of narrative for developing skills of critique about the professional self and professional practice (Bold, 2012). The importance of researching from the inside to develop a sense-of-self personally and professionally (Mason, 1994) is central to self-reflection.

The power of reflective writing informs reflective practice and professional learning and development; reflection creates a film-like dialogue with the self (Bolton, 2010). An observation, conversation, a critical incident, a journal or diary extract or a piece of writing might support the creation of a personal reflective narrative (Bold, 2012). Writing stories is a way professional learners can set up an internal dialogue for reflective inquiry and practice (Hughes, 2009). By reflecting upon personal and professional life-histories, practitioners and leaders are able to make sense of influences and construct values, beliefs and pedagogy for working with children and families and in leadership roles. These 'lived experiences' and lived relationships are personal and professional journeys (Clough and Corbett, 2000: 156). From critically reflecting upon, deconstructing and reconstructing these experiences, relationships, significant events and influences, professional identity and self-perception emerges from personal and professional knowledge and understanding.

Personal narratives are enquiries about the self, the personal and professional aspects of leaders and practitioners' life-histories are intertwined, giving each other significance and contributing to the development of professional identity (Court et al., 2009). In New Zealand, there is a view that the learning self is the basis for professionalism, the engagement with people, things, ideas, policies and politics as part of an ongoing discourse (Duhn, 2011). In Sinclair's (2011) work on leadership identity, a commitment to reflective learning, experiential process learning and applying critical perspectives was important to understanding identity. Learning is developed through experience and inquiry, informing reflective practice (Paige-Smith and Craft, 2011). Reflective practice is described by Appleby (2010) as a never-ending learning journey and Bolton (2010) describes learning journeys as *stories of experience*.

Stories of leadership experience

The concept of stories-of-experience and discovery was applied to the emerging understanding of early years leadership and identity during a workshop session on a master's-level course about leading policy and practice for early childhood services for existing leaders working in the early years sector. Influenced by the work of Aubrey (2011), who traced leaders' practical paths or journeys into leadership, the leaders were asked to represent their professional journey into leadership and their leadership identity through visual representation, reflective writing and dialogue with others to make meaning and sense of their lived leadership experience. The narratives provided a retrospective examination of key influences and events (Court et al., 2009) that impacted upon the women's development as early years leaders. Each woman's story of leadership experience produced a uniquely personal collection of information; reflection enabled a profound insight into personal and professional feelings, values, beliefs and attitudes about their leadership development and identity (Croft et al., 2009). The narrative telling of their stories, the story structure, its language and characteristics, revealed much about the storyteller and her craft of telling and living her life (Ashrat-Pink, 2008).

The following three case studies are stories-of-experience of women early years leaders reflecting upon their journeys of leadership and who they are as leaders, highlighting influences and events along the way. The first two case studies focus upon each leader's journey into leadership and their leadership identity; in the third case study the leader reflects upon her leadership journey, development and practices. The leaders' drawings and writing are used as authentic voices of effective and caring leaders working in the early years.

Case study: Flo's leadership story

In an extract from Flo's reflective journal, she reflects upon her journey to becoming an early years leader of a Foundation Stage unit in a large primary school and illustrates her leadership identity.

I had been an Early Years Teacher for many years and was quite happy working with the children. I wasn't really looking to become a leader. I was 'head-hunted' to apply for the leadership post of Foundation Stage Coordinator in the primary school to work with the senior management team for the school's forthcoming Ofsted inspection. I was head of the nursery in an independent school and encouraged by my deputy head to apply for the larger leadership role. I was studying a master's degree in early years education; this filled me with inspiration and confidence to apply. During the course, I studied a module about early years leadership, the tutor asked us to reflect upon our leadership style and practices, and to represent our leadership identity in an illustration.

I illustrated my leadership as a willow tree (Figure 11.1), with a trunk and branches that move in a flexible way, the leaves gently moving in the wind overhanging and reflecting in a clear lake of water. I reflect upon my leadership at times so I can be flexible to meet the differing needs of the school, the Foundation Stage unit, the staff, parents and children. I find time and space for this; the changes in the early years sector seem to be blowing through the leaves and I need time to think about these and consider the best way forward for our setting.

The willow tree sways over the lake but doesn't fall in as it is secured by strong roots of service, experience, knowledge, values, pedagogy and best practice. My interpersonal qualities of compassion, courage, respect, patience and emotional intelligence are approaches used in my leadership practice and interactions with staff, parents, children and other professionals.

To summarize, who am I as a leader? I'm a flexible and reflective leader grounded in early years knowledge, pedagogy and practice.

(Continues)

(Continued)

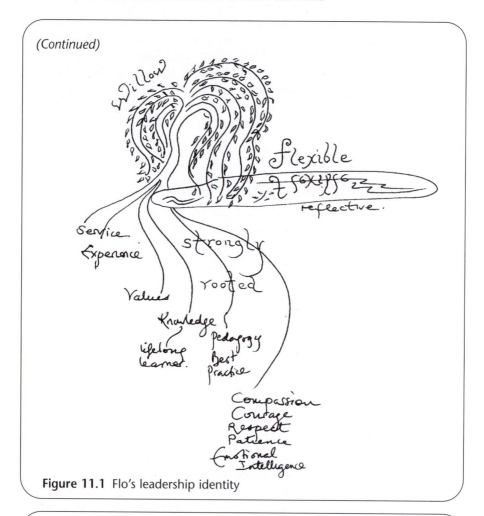

Figure 11.1 Flo's leadership identity

📁 Case study: Alison's leadership story

Alison is a graduate early years leader of a private daycare provision, a workplace nursery providing early education and childcare for the children of employees.

In my reading of Carol Aubrey and Jillian Rodd's work it has been suggested that leaders in early years settings do not easily relate to the role of a leader or see themselves as such. Furthermore, leaders don't have a clear pathway to follow and receive little training for leading others. Leadership was a role of natural progression. I was offered a leadership role without being given help or advice and I took it without thought to develop my leadership skills.

Leadership is developed on shared understandings in a given time and place. In my first leadership experience, I was required to lead a room, the curriculum, pedagogy and practice within the room but not to manage staff. In my second leadership experience in another setting I was expected to lead the room, curriculum and staff, acting as their line manager; I had greater autonomy in this setting.

I felt that I needed some leadership training and the introduction of the graduate early years leadership award (EYPS) as a driver to raise quality of provision and act as a change agent came at the right time for me. Achieving the EYPS award didn't alter my role in any way but I developed confidence to lead and support others in their pedagogy and practice. As a graduate early years leader, an Early Years Professional, I have never found my identity as a professional questioned, rather my skills have been recognized as standalone qualities.

In illustrating my leadership identity (Figure 11.2), I realize that effective leadership is complex and can be challenging at times.

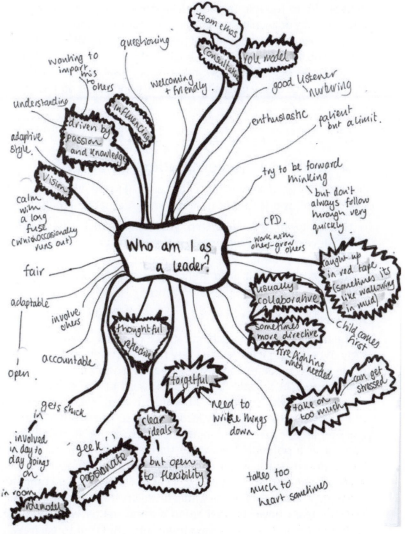

Figure 11.2 Alison's leadership identity   (Continues)

(Continued)

In reflecting upon who I am as a leader, I seem to have many aspects to my leadership style and practices. The aspects circled seem to be the most important to me; *driven by passion and knowledge; thoughtful and reflective, having clear ideals but being open to flexibility; visionary; consultative; influencing; being a role model and demonstrating to others.* I can also be *caught up in red tape (sometimes it's like wallowing in mud); take on too much and can get stressed; be forgetful; usually collaborative but sometimes more directive.* These are the ups and downs of being a leader in a busy early years setting.

As a leader I endeavour to be open, fair and consistent. I aim to develop both myself and my team; recognizing that not only is it a prerequisite to the role to continually develop one's knowledge but it is a key way of keeping passion alive for Early Childhood Education. I have grown as a leader in understanding my capabilities through Continuing Professional Development, reflection and practical leadership experiences. I am now able to lead collaboratively and have the confidence in my own abilities and lead others to do the same.

 ## Case study: Michelle's leadership story

Michelle's story of leadership experience (Figure 11.3) shows her development as a leader in national and international contexts.

To reflect upon her leadership journey, Michelle used Bloom's (1997) development framework of the three stages of a director of leader's development – a beginning leader, a competent leader and a master leader – as it accurately represents the process she went through as a leader in a primary school.

A beginning leader

At the beginning of my teaching career, I never considered the possibility of becoming a leader. The very notion of traditional leadership, a sole leader, made me opposed to the very idea. I became an accidental leader or a leader by chance, it was not something I chose consciously; it was something I became through circumstance as is the case of many early years leaders. Like so many other leaders I received little leadership training. However, my professional development as a potential leader was strengthened at the start of my career due to the passion and commitment of the school's early years coordinator. She was an excellent role model, clear communicator and inspired confidence within her team. It was her relationships with the team however, that stood out; no matter what pressures were placed on her, she always found time to listen to each team

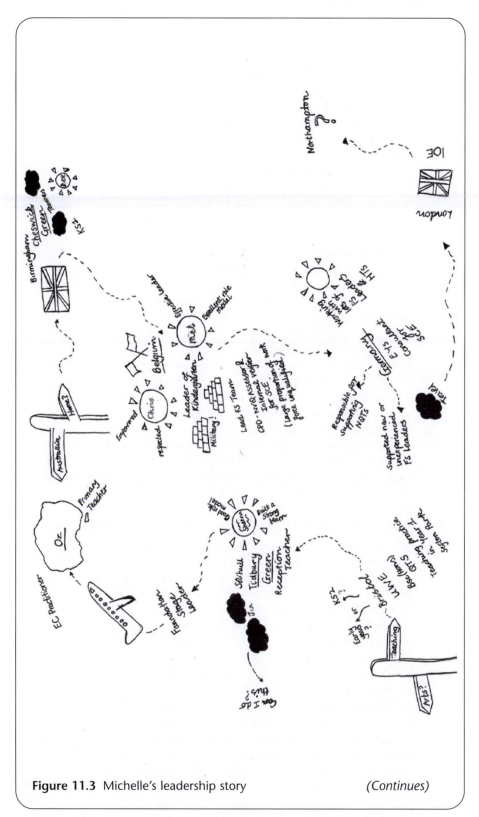

Figure 11.3 Michelle's leadership story   *(Continues)*

(Continued)

member and everyone thought highly of her. She taught me about the importance of forming good relationships.

I was asked to take over the responsibility for coordinating the Foundation Stage. I decided to accept the position. This gave me a small taste of leadership but not a breadth of experience as I didn't need to build a team; I was inheriting a team that was well established and had a clear vision for developing quality provision which had been built through distributive effective leadership of my predecessor. My role as a leader during this period was more about monitoring developments against identified goals. However, what that experience did was to challenge my initial opposition to becoming a leader and the misconceptions of what being a leader was all about.

The terms leadership and management are frequently interchanged and are part of the early years leader's role but there is confusion about where one starts and the other begins. The confusion created by this terminology was reflected in my own experiences when I ventured into a leadership role again in a British primary school for service children in Belgium. As a Foundation Stage Manager I had responsibility for the day-to-day running of the early years unit as well as a teaching commitment in the reception class. My job description stated that I was responsible for the management of the financial, human and material resources within the 56-place setting. However, on arrival my other responsibility was to raise standards in the quality of teaching and learning in the early years. Hence I was not just a manager but a leader too. What was evident from my experience is the clear difference between the roles of leadership and management. The manager has the role of organizing and coordinating the workforce and has responsibility for the organization's day-to-day effectiveness. The leader, in contrast, provides direction, inspires, is responsible for team-building and is a role model for the workforce.

The workforce of this Foundation Stage unit in Belgium was diverse and complex. One of the biggest challenges was that the workforce was recruited from local British military community who resided there for short periods of time. This led to regular staff changes and little continuity within the early years team. I became the consistent continuity. The workforce was made up of a team of largely unqualified and inexperienced women seeking employment whilst their husbands were posted overseas. This presented a huge challenge; there was a continuous and ongoing need to professionalize the workforce. Hence I needed a thorough training programme, a clear induction procedure and to be able to support them in achieving relevant and recognized qualifications to meet statutory requirements.

In terms of my own leadership training, like many teachers my initial teacher training was concerned far more with my subject specialism rather than supporting me as a potential leader. I felt confident as a teacher and in my understanding about what constituted high-quality teaching and learning. What I needed was support in the transition from managing children to managing and leading adults. To be an effective leader, I also needed to be committed and competent in training the workforce; to have an understanding of mentoring and coaching skills, an ability to facilitate professional development and an ethos which promoted professional discussion. Despite my lack of leadership preparation in my teacher training, my first experience of coordinating a Foundation Stage had given me a valuable insight into a way of approaching leadership through being a distributive leader. What I was unclear about was how to go about achieving this and whether this model could be achieved within the context of a military service school. I needed to take into account the context in which I was working. The military community in which I worked was fundamentally a male-orientated world and of course steeped in a tradition of hierarchical leadership. I was concerned this community held a view of a leader as someone who displayed masculine traits, who was conformist, competitive and authoritative rather than a leader who sought to be collaborative, cooperative and promoted teamwork. If this view was held, implementing a distributed model of leadership would be challenging, particularly as it required the involvement of everyone within the team to influence and inspire one another to bring about change, rather than one person to dictate what that change was to be.

During my first year as the leader and manager of the Foundation Stage, I was continually concerned about whether I was capable of supporting all learners within the setting. Like Bloom suggests, all beginning leaders question their adequacy, I was also concerned about fitting in and being liked by this team of phenomenally strong women. This caused me to initially place most emphasis on building relationships with the team.

A competent leader

It took me two years to make the transition from a beginning leader to that of the competent leader. As Bloom suggests, I went from a stage of struggling to that of juggling and became more focused on the job in hand; raising the quality of provision in the setting. A number of factors influenced this change. What made the biggest impact to the quality of the workforce was staff being able to gain a National Vocational Qualification (NVQ) whilst working. I achieved the NVQ Assessor's award and this enabled me to have a hands-on approach to supporting the staff's professional development through regular observation, feedback and target-setting. Gaining a qualification was a massive achievement for some of these women, many of whom had left school with few qualifications and whose lives were heavily dictated by their husband's career. Through their qualifications these

(Continues)

(Continued)

women gained in confidence both personally and professionally and there was a sense of empowerment around them, and they began to acknowledge their job as their career that they would pursue when they returned to the UK.

This marked the start of empowerment for me as a leader; I felt empowered by empowering others. I began critically reflecting more on my own practice and that of the setting but more importantly I considered the impact that practice was having on children's achievement, their dispositions to learning and well-being. This process had a significant impact on formulating a vision that was specific to the needs of the children and the setting, rather than the one I had as a beginning leader, which was built on government policy.

As the staff were growing in confidence, they were beginning to reflect and make suggestions on how provision could be enhanced. This was a turning point, and to facilitate this further it was important to recognize their ideas, allow them to use their initiative, show their judgement was trusted and provide opportunities for leadership. This created an ethos where they were more open to change. So rather than the setting's aim being based on my vision, what was emerging was the development of a team vision. This was a significant step forward as collection reflection is central in enabling organizational change. It also appears my desire to develop a distributive model of leadership was being realized in a climate of trust and openness.

Through creating a sense of empowerment, there was a sense of ownership and responsibility in the team. I wanted to develop this culture to pedagogy for children's learning. I presented my ideas about empowering children, giving them more choice and ownership of their learning, using their ideas and interests to lead the curriculum in a child-centred way, so they would have a far greater disposition to learn. I was asked by the head teacher to develop an action plan that had a realistic time-frame to bring about change and clear ways that progress could be monitored. I recognized that to be successful it would need to involve everyone within the team. I was concerned that for some staff it may feel overwhelming with a shift from a prescriptive way of working to one that was far freer. One of the ways that I attempted to overcome this was to ensure that everyone was equally involved in the planning and decision-making stages and that they viewed the change as challenge and not threatening; by understanding the need for change and being involved in the change process the change would more likely be successful. For me as a leader, reflection played a key role in implementing change as I continuously evaluated what was working well and what needed to be further enhanced.

As the setting's practice developed from strength to strength as a result of the dedication and drive of all team members we were asked to share practice with others. The sharing of practice across school's and the establishment of professional learning communities supports the development of schools, raises standards and gives professional development opportunities for staff to share practice with other teachers and educators.

A master leader

It was after four years in my role and I had grown in confidence as a leader that I became what Bloom describes as a 'master director or leader'. At this stage, I understood my role as a change agent, and felt confident to handle virtually any situation. The workforce in the military school continued to be transient; I developed systems for staff recruitment, induction and appraisal. Some practitioners joined the team with prior experience, bringing fresh ideas about how provision and practice could be advanced.

I recognize myself as a motivating leader because I finally achieved equal emphasis on both relationships and getting the task in hand completed. I feel confident in decision-making and problem-solving, confident in the abilities of staff, endeavouring to ensure all staff are involved in policy-making and goal-setting. I increasingly have the confidence to take risks.

Concluding thoughts

My leadership experience over my teaching career has highlighted the importance of some significant factors. There is a need for future potential leaders and new leaders to receive relevant training and support. Although this has been promoted through new higher education awards such as the EYPS and NPQICL, it also needs to be addressed in initial teacher training.

During my leadership journey, being a 'beginning leader' was a time of considerable challenge and isolation due to my lack of preparation for the role. However, it illustrates how challenges that I faced in my leadership role strengthened me as a leader. One of the most crucial factors in supporting my leadership success was my ability to critically reflect on my own practice and within a learning community. During my time as a leader, reflection became a continuous process that supported the development of children, staffs' learning and my leadership learning. As I start the next phase of my career as university lecturer, I will take this with me.

Flo's, Alison's and Michelle's leadership stories have provided a reflective insight into effective and caring leadership in the early years. Their leadership practices demonstrate the leadership themes and practices discussed in Part 2 of this book: directional, collaborative, empowering and pedagogical.

You may like to reflect upon your own story-of-experience, your leadership story and journey, identity and practices through a pictorial and written representation.

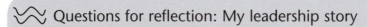 Questions for reflection: My leadership story

Provide yourself with a table, paper, a range of pens, pencils, crayons and felt-tipped pens; use these to visually represent aspects of your leadership story by drawing an image. The suggestions below may help you to focus upon an aspect of your leadership story of experience:

- Your journey into leadership, showing key events and influences along the way.
- Who am I? Illustrate your identity as a leader, your leadership style and practices.

Use this visual representation as the basis for reflection, reflectively write about your leadership story. Using a laptop to write will add speed to the reflective process. As you write don't worry about spelling and punctuation, the process of writing provides reflective time and space for you to consider your leadership story. Alternatively you could reflectively dialogue with another existing or aspiring leader. These questions provide a starting point for reflection.

- How did the key events and influences impact upon your development as a leader?
- How did the key events and influences impact upon your leadership style and practices?
- What leadership theories or writers have influenced your leadership practice or identity?

 Summary

In this concluding chapter, effective and caring leadership practices are illustrated and demonstrated through lived experiences of leadership through narrative exploration. Three early childhood leaders share their autobiographical reflective stories-of-experience, their leadership journeys, and understandings of their identity as leaders, leadership styles and practices. Their stories demonstrate the leadership themes and practices of directional, collaborative, empowering and pedagogical leadership in the Model of Effective and Caring Leadership Practices discussed earlier in Part 2 of the book. There was opportunity for existing and aspiring leaders to similarly illustrate and explore their leadership story-of-experience through autobiographical narrative and reflection.

Further reading

Aubrey, C. (2011) 'Journeys into leadership', in C. Aubrey, *Leading and Managing in the Early Years*. 2nd edn. London: Sage. pp. 78–88.
   This chapter traces leaders' practical paths and journeys into leadership and explores the support needed at different points in a leadership career trajectory as beginning, competent and master leaders.
Court, D., Merva, L. and Oran, E. (2009) 'Pre-school teachers' narratives: a window on personal-professional history, values and beliefs', *International Journal of Early Years Education*, 17(3): 395–406.
   This journal article examines the use of narrative in teachers' professional understanding.
Hallet, E. (2013) *The Reflective Early Years Practitioner*. London: Sage. pp. 125–52.
   In chapter 9, 'Reflective learning journeys', through autobiographical storying, women graduates reflect upon their learning journey through higher education. In chapter 10, 'Continuing learning pathways and future reflections', the contribution of graduate practitioners' knowledge and research in influencing change in provision and practice is examined through autobiographical storying.
Hughes, G. (2009) 'Talking to oneself: using autobiographical internal dialogue to critique everyday and professional practice', *Reflective Practice*, 10(4): 451–63.
   This journal article examines the use of reflection in autobiographical study.
Sinclair, A. (2011) 'Being leaders: identities and identity work in leadership', in A. Bryman, D. Collinson, D. Grint, B. Jackson and M. Uhl-Bien (eds), *The Sage Handbook of Leadership*. London: Sage. pp. 508–17.
   In this chapter, the author describes her work within workshops in exploring leadership identity.

References

Abbott, L. and Nutbrown, C. (eds) (2001) *Experiencing Reggio Emilia: Implications for Pre-school Provision*. Buckingham: Open University Press.

Aguirre Jones, D. and Elders, L. (2009) '5x5x5 = creativity in practice', in S. Bancroft, M. Fawcett and P. Hay (eds), *Researching Children: Researching the World 5x5x5 = Creativity*. Stoke-on-Trent: Trentham Books. pp. 12–13.

Allen, G. (2011) *Early Intervention: The Next Steps*. (Allen Review.) London: Her Majesty's Government.

Anderson, M., Gronn, P., Ingvarson, L., Jackson, A., Kleinhenz, E., McKenzie, P., Mulford, B. and Thornton, N. (2007) 'Australia: country background report – OECD improving school leadership activity', report prepared for the Australian Government Department of Education, Science and Training, Australian Council for Educational Research (ACER), Melbourne, Australia.

Anning, A. and Edwards, A. (2003) 'The inquiring professional', in A. Anning and A. Edwards (eds), *Promoting Children's Learning from Birth to Five*. Buckingham: Open University Press. pp. 35–58.

Appleby, K. (2010) 'Reflective thinking: reflective practice', in M. Reed and N. Canning (eds), *Reflective Practice in the Early Years*. London: Sage. pp. 7–23.

Arvizu, S. (1996) 'Family, community, and school collaboration', in J. Sikula (ed.), *Handbook of Research on Teacher Education*. New York: Simon and Schuster Macmillan.

Ashrat-Pink , I. (2008) in Court, D., Merav, L. and Oran, E. (2009) 'Pre-school teachers' narratives: a window on personal-professional history, values and beliefs', *International Journal of Early Years Education*, 17(3): 211.

Aubrey, C. (2011) *Leading and Managing in the Early Years*. 2nd edn. London: Sage.

Baldock, P., Fitzgerald, D. and Kay, J. (2013) *Understanding Early Years Policy*. 3rd edn. London: Sage.

Ball, C. (1994) *Start Right: The Importance of Early Learning*. London: RSA.

Barnett, W.S. (2004) 'Better teachers, better preschools: student achievement linked to teacher qualifications', *Preschool Policy Matters*, issue 2. New Brunswick, NJ: NIEER.

Bass, B.N. (1985) *Leadership and Performance beyond Expectations*. New York: Free Press.

Baumfield, V.M. (2013) 'Pedagogy', in D. Wyse, V.M. Baumfield, D. Egan, C. Gallagher, L. Hayward, M. Hulme, R. Leitch, K. Livingston, I. Menter and B. Lingard (eds), *Creating the Curriculum*. London: Routledge. pp. 46–58.

Bennett, N., Wise, C., Woods, P. and Harvey, J. (2003) *Distributed Leadership: A Literature Review*. Nottingham: National College for School Leadership.

Bennis, W. and Nanus, B. (1997) *Leaders: Strategies for Taking Charge*. Cambridge, MA: Harvard Business Review Press.

Blackmore, J. (1999) *Troubling Women: Feminism, Leadership and Educational Change*. Buckingham: Open University Press.

Bloom, P.J. (1997) 'Navigating the rapids: directors reflect upon their careers and professional development', *Young Children*, 52(7): 32–8.

Bold, C. (2012) *Using Narrative in Research*. London: Sage.

Bolton, G. (2010) *Reflective Practice: Writing and Professional Development*. 3rd edn. London: Sage.

Bowlby, J. (1988) *A Secure Base: Clinical Applications of Attachement Theory*. Oxford: Routledge.

Bruce, T. (2006) *Early Childhood: A Guide for Students*. London: Sage.

Bubb, S. and Earley, P. (2007) *Leading and Managing Continuing Professional Development*. 2nd edn. London: Paul Chapman Publishing.

Bush, T. and Glover, D. (2003) *School Leadership: Concepts and Evidence. Summary Report*. Nottingham: National College for School Leadership.

Bush, T. (2011) *Theories of Educational Leadership and Management*. 4th edn. London: Sage.

Bush, T., Bell, L. and Middlewood, D. (2010) *The Principles of Educational Leadership and Management*. London: Sage.

Cameron, C. (2001) 'Promise or problem? A review of the literature on men working in early childhood services', *Gender Work and Organisation*, 8(4): 430–53.

Chan, L.K.S. and Mellor, E.J. (2002) (eds) *International Developments in Early Childhood Services*. New York: Peter Lang.

Charmaz, K. (2005) 'Grounded theory in the 21st century', in N.K. Denzin and Y.S. Lincoln (eds), *Qualitative Research*. 3rd edn. London: Sage. pp. 507–35.

Children's Workforce Development Council (CWDC) (2006) *A Headstart for All: Early Years Professional Status: Candidate Information*. Leeds: CWDC.

Children's Workforce Development Council (CWDC) (2008) *Introduction and Information Guide: Early Years Professionals, Creating Brighter Futures*. Leeds: Children's Workforce Development Council.

Chrisholm, L. (2001) 'Gender and leadership in South African educational administration', *Gender and Education*, 13(4): 387–99.

Clough, P. and Corbett, J. (2000) *Theories of Inclusive Education*. London: Paul Chapman.

Coleman, M. (2008) 'Annotated bibliography: support and development of women leaders at work'. London: Work-based Learning Centre, Institute of Education, University of London.

Coleman, M. (2011) *Women at the Top: Challenges, Choice and Change*. Basingstoke: Palgrave Macmillan.

Colley, H. (2006) 'Learning to labour with feeling: class, gender and emotion in childcare education and training', *Contemporary Issues in Early Childhood*, 7(1): 15–29.

Colloby, J. (2009) *The Validation Process for EYPS*. 2nd edn. Exeter: Learning Matters.

Colmer, K. (2008) 'Leading a learning organisation: Australian early years centres as learning networks', *European Early Childhood Education Research Journal*, 16(1): 107–15.

Costley, C. and Armsby, P. (2007) 'Work-based learning assessed as a mode of study', *Assessment and Evaluation in Higher Education*, 32(1): 21–33.

Cottle, M. and Alexander, E. (2012) 'Quality in early years settings: government, research and practitioners' perspectives', *British Educational Research Journal*, 38(4): pp. 635–54.

Court, D., Merva, L. and Oran, E. (2009) 'Pre-school teachers' narratives: a window on personal-professional history, values and beliefs', *International Journal of Early Years Education*, 17(3): pp. 395–406.

Cushman, P. (2005) 'It's just not a real bloke's job: male teachers in the primary school', *Asia-Pacific Journal of Teacher Education*, 33(3): 321–38.

Dalli, C. (2008) 'Pedagogy, knowledge and collaboration: towards a ground-up perspective on professionalism', *European Early Childhood Research Journal, Special Issue: Professionalism in Early Childhood Education and Care*, 16(2): 171–85.

Davis, J.M. and Smith, M. (2012) *Working in Multi-professional Contexts*. London: Sage.

De Graf, S., Bosman, A., Hasselman, F. and Verhoevan, L. (2009) 'Benefits of systematic phonics instruction', *Scientific Studies of Reading*, 13(4): 318–33.

Den Hartog, D.N., House, R.J., Hanges, P.J. and Ruiz-Quintanilla, S.A. (1999) 'Culture specific and cross culturally generalizable implicit leadership theories: are attributes of charismatic/transformational leadership universally endorsed?', *The Leadership Quarterly*, 10(2): 219–56.

Department for Children, Schools and Families (DCSF) (2006) *The Independent Review of the Teaching of Early Reading*. (Rose Report.) Nottingham: DCSF.

Department for Children, Schools and Families (DCSF) (2007) *National Standards for Leaders of SureStart Children's Centres*. Nottingham: DCSF Publications.

Department for Children, Schools and Families (DCSF) (2008a) *2020 Children and Young People's Workforce Strategy*. London: DCSF.

Department for Children, Schools and Families (DCSF) (2008b) *Statutory Framework for the Early Years Foundation Stage*. Nottingham: DCSF.

Department for Education (DfE) (2011) *Evaluation of the Graduate Leader Fund: Final Report*. DFE-RR144. London: DFE

Department for Education (2012) *Foundations for Quality: The Independent Review of Early Education and Childcare Qualifications: Final Report*. (Nutbrown Review). Available at www.education.gov.uk. (accessed September 2012).

Department for Education (DfE) (2013) *More Great Childcare*. (Truss Report.) London: DfE.

Department for Education and Science (DES) (1990) *Starting With Quality: The Rumbold Report*. London: Her Majesty's Stationery Office.

Department for Education and Skills (DfES) (2004a) 'Statisitics of education: school workforce in England', available at: www.dfes.gov.uk, accessed 2004.

Department for Education and Skills (DfES) (2004b) *Every Child Matters: Change for Children*. DfES 1081/2004. London: DfES.

Department for Education and Skills (DfES) (2005a) *Children's Workforce Strategy*. Nottingham: DfES Publications.

Department for Education and Skills (DfES) (2005b) 'Championing children: a shared set of skills, knowledge and behaviours for managers of integrated children's service', draft paper. Nottingham: DfES Publications.

Department for Education and Skills (DfES) (2005c) *Common Core of Skills for the Children's Workforce*. Nottingham. DfES Publications.

Desforges, C. and Abouchaar, A. (2003) *The Impact of Parental Involvement, Parental Support and Family Education on Pupil Achievements and Adjustments: A Literature Review*. London: DfES.

Diaz-Saenz, H.R. (2011) 'Transformational leadership', in A. Bryman, D. Collinson, D. Grint, B. Jackson and M. Uhl-Bien (eds), *The Sage Handbook of Leadership*. London: Sage. pp. 299–337.

Draper, L. and Duffy, B. (2010) 'Working with parents', in C. Cable, L. Miller and G. Goodliff (eds), *Working with Children in the Early Years*. 2nd edn. London: Paul Chapman. pp. 268–79.

Duffy, B. and Marshall, J. (2007) 'Leadership in multi-agency work', in I. Siraj-Blatchford, K. Clarke and M. Needham (eds), *The Team Around the Child: Multi-agency Working in the Early Years*. Stoke-on-Trent: Trentham Books. pp. 105–120.

Dufour, R. (2004) 'Cultural shift doesn't occur overnight – or without conflict', *National Staff Development Council*, 25(4). London: National Staff Development Council.

Duhn, I. (2011) 'Towards professionalism/s', in. L. Miller and C. Cable (eds), *Professionalisation, Leadership and Management in the Early Years*. London: Sage. pp. 133–46.

Elfer, P. (2012) 'Emotion in nursery work: work discussion as a model of critical professional reflection', *Early Years: An International Journal of Research and Development*, 32(2): pp. 129–41.

Ellsworth, A. (2005) *Places of Learning: Media, Architecture, Pedagogy*. New York: RoutledgeFalmer.

Epstein, J. (1986) 'Parents' reactions to teacher practices of parent involvement', *Elementary School Journal*, 86: 278–94.

Fairhurst, G.T. (2011) 'Discursive approaches to leadership', in A. Bryman, D. Collinson, K. Grint, B. Jackson and M. Uhl-Bien (eds), *The Sage Handbook of Leadership*. London: Sage. pp. 495–507.

Fitzgerald, T. and Gunter, H. (2008) 'Contesting the orthodoxy of teacher leadership', *International Journal of School Leadership*, 11(4): 331–40.

Field, F. (2010) *The Foundation Years: Preventing Poor Children Becoming Poor Adults*. London: Her Majesty's Government.

Foot, H., Howe, C., Cheyne, B., Terras, B. and Rattray, C. (2002) 'Parental participation and partnership in pre-school provision', *International Journal of Early Years Education*, 10(1): pp. 5–19.

Friedman, R. (2007) 'Professionalism in the early years', in M. Wild and H. Mitchell (eds), *Early Childhood Studies: A Reflective Reader*. Exeter: Learning Matters. pp. 124–9.

Garrick, R. and Morgan, A. (2009) 'The children's centre teacher role: developing practice in the private, voluntary and independent sector', *Early Years: An International Journal of Research and Development*, 29(1): 69–81.

Geertz, C. (1973) 'Thick description: towards an interpretive theory of culture', in C. Geertz, *The Interpretation of Cultures*. New York: Falmer.

Gilligan, C. (1982) *In a Different Voice*. Cambridge, MA: Harvard University Press.

Gold, A., Evans, J., Earley, P., Halpin, D. and Collarbone, P. (2002) 'Principled principals? Values-driven leadership: evidence from ten case studies of "outstanding" school leaders', paper presented at the Annual Meeting of the American Educational Research association, New Orleans, USA, April.

Goleman, D. (1996) *Emotional Intelligence: Why It Can Matter More than IQ*. London: Bloomsbury Paperbacks.

Goleman, D. (2002) *The New Leaders*. London: Time Warner.

Greenfield, S. (2011) 'Working in multi-disciplinary teams', in L. Miller and C. Cable (eds), *Professionalization, Leadership and Management in the Early Years*. London: Sage. pp. 77–90.

Greenleaf, R.K. (2003) *The Servant-Leader within a Transformational Path*. New York: Pailist Press.

Gronn, P. (2002) 'Distributed leadership', in K. Leithwood, P. Hallinger, K. Seashore-Louis, G. Furman-Brown, P. Gronn, W. Mulford and K. Riley (eds), *Second International Handbook of Educational Leadership and Administration*. Dordrecht: Kluwer. pp. 614–53.

Groundwater-Smith, S. and Sachs. J. (2002) 'The activist professional and the reinstatement of trust', *Cambridge Journal of Education*, 32(3): 341–58.

Guile, D. and Lucas, N. (1999) 'Rethinking initial teacher education and professional development in further education: towards the learning professional', in A. Green and N. Lucas (eds), *Further Education and Lifelong Learning: Realigning the Sector for the Twenty-first Century*. London: Bedford Way Papers, Institute of Education.

Hadfield, M., Jopling, M., Waller, T. and Emira, M. (2011) 'Longitudinal study of early years professional status: interim report 14 March 2011', University of Wolverhampton.

Hallet, E. (2013) *The Reflective Early Years Practitioner*. London: Sage.

Hallet, E. (2014) *Leadership of Learning in Early Years Practice*. London: Institute of Education Press.

Hallet, E. and Roberts-Holmes, G. (2010) *Research into the Contribution of the Early Years Professional Status Role to Quality Improvement Strategies in Gloucestershire: Final Report*. London: Institute of Education, University of London.

Handy, C. (1990) *Inside Organisations*. London: BBC Books.

Harpley, A. and Roberts, A. (2006) *You Can Survive Your Early Years OFSTED Inspection*. Leamington Spa: Scholastic.

Harris, A. (2002) 'Distributed leadership in schools: leading or misleading', keynote paper, Belmas Conference.

Hatcher, R. (2005) 'The distribution of leadership and power in schools', *British Journal of Sociology of Education*, 26(2): 253–67.

Hayden, J. (1997) 'Directors of early childhood services: experiences, preparedness and selection', *Australian Research in Early Childhood*, 1(1): 49–67.

Hopkins, D. (2005) 'System leadership', seminar presentation to the London Centre for Leadership in Learning, Institute of Education, University of London, 12 December.

Hughes, G. (2009) 'Talking to oneself: using autobiographical internal dialogue to critique everyday and professional practice', *Reflective Practice*, 10(4): 451–63.

Jackson, D. (2003) 'Foreword', in A. Harris and L. Lambert, *Building Leadership Capacity for School Improvement*. Maidenhead: Open University Press. pp. x–xxiii.

Jones, C. and Pound, L. (2008) *Leadership and Management in the Early Years*. Maidenhead: Open University Press.

Jonsdottir, A.H. and Hard, L. (2009) 'Leadership in early childhood in Iceland and Australia: diversities in culture yet similarities in challenges', paper presented at European Early Childhood Education Research Association (EECERA) conference, Stravanger, Norway, September.

Jung, D., Yammarino, F.J. and Lee, J. K. (2009) 'Moderating role of subordinates' attitudes on transformational leadership and effectiveness: a multi-cultural perspective', *Leadership Quarterly*, 20(4): 586–603.

Kagan, S.L. and Hallmark, L.G. (2001) 'Cultivating leadership in early care and education', *Childcare Information Exchange*, 140: 7–10.

Kavanagh, M.H. and Ashkanasy, N.M. (2006) 'The impact of leadership and change management strategy on organizational culture and individual acceptance during a merger', *British Journal of Management*, 17: 81–103.

Knowles, G. (2009) *Ensuring Every Child Matters*. London: Sage.

Kouzes, J.M. and Posner, B.Z. (2007) *The Leadership Challenge*. 4th edn. San Francisco, CA: Jossey-Bass.

Leithwood, K. and Levin, B. (2005) 'Assessing school leader and leadership programme effects on pupil learning: conceptual and methodological problems', research report RR662. Nottingham: DfES.

Leithwood, K. and Riehl, C. (2003) 'What do we already know about successful school leadership', AREA division: a task force on developing research in educational leadership, accessed at: http://www.cepa.gse.rutgers.edu/whatweknow. pdf, accessed 2007.

Lingard, B., Hayes, D., Mills, M. and Christie, P. (2003) *Leading Learning: Making Hope Practical in Schools*. Maidenhead: Open University Press.

Lloyd, E. and Hallet, E. (2010) 'Professionalizing the early childhood workforce in England: work in progress or missed opportunity?', *Contemporary Issues in Early Childhood*, 11(1): 75–87.

Lord, P., Sharpe, C., Jeffes, J. and Grayson, H. (2011) 'Review of the literature on effective leadership in children's centres and foundation years' system leadership. Report for the National College for School Leadership', unpublished report, National Foundation for Educational Research, Slough.

Lumby, J. and Coleman, M. (2007) *Leadership and Diversity: Challenging Theory and Practice in Education*. London: Sage.

Luthans, F. and Avolio, B. (2003) 'Authentic leadership development', in K.S. Cameron, J.E. Dutton and R.E. Quinn (eds), *Positive Organisational Scholarship*. San Francisco, CA: Berrett-Koehler, pp. 241–3.

MacBeath, J. (2003) 'The alphabet soup of leadership', in *Inform No. 2*. Cambridge: University of Cambridge Faculty of Education. pp. 1–7.

MacLeod-Brudenell, I. (2008) 'Trends and traditions in early years education and care', in I. MacLeod-Brudenell and J. Kay (eds), *Advanced Early Years*. 2nd edn. London: Pearson. pp. 15–40.

MacNeill, N., Cavanagh, R., Dellar, G. and Silcox, S. (2004) 'The principalship and pedagogical leadership', paper presented at the American Educational Research Association Annual Meeting, San Diego.

Manning-Morton, J. (2006) 'The personal is professional: professionalism and the birth to threes practitioner', *Contemporary Issues in Early Childhood*, 7(1): 42–52.

Marmot, M. (2010) 'Marmot Review report – fair society, healthy lives', available at: www.idea.gov.uk, accessed 27 September 2011.

Mason, J. (1994) *Researching From the Inside in Mathematical Education: Locating an I-You Relationship*. Centre for Mathematics Education. Milton Keynes: Open University.

Mazutis, D. and Slawinski, N. (2008). 'Leading organizational learning through authentic dialogue', *Management Learning*, 39(4): 437–56.

McCall, C. and Lawlor, H. (2000) *School Leadership: Leadership Examined*. London: The Stationery Office.

McDowall Clark, R. (2010) 'I never thought of myself as a leader … reconceptualising leadership with EYPS', conference paper 20th EECERA Conference, Birmingham, 6–8 September.

McDowall Clark, R. (2012) '"I've never thought of myself as a leader but ...": the early years professional and catalytic leadership', *European Early Childhood Education Research Journal*, 20(3): 391–401.

McDowall Clark, R. and Murray, J. (2012) *Reconceptualizing Leadership in the Early Years*. Maidenhead: Open University Press.

McMillan, D.J (2009) 'Preparing for educare: student perspectives on early years training in Northern Ireland', *International Journal of Early Years Education*, 17(3): 219–35.

Miller, K. (2006) 'Introduction: women in leadership and management: progress thus far?', in D. McTavish and K. Miller (eds), *Women in Leadership and Management*. Cheltenham: Edward Elgar.

Miller, L. and Cable, C. (2008) *Professionalism in the Early Years*. Abingdon: Hodder Education.

Moon, J. (1999) *Reflection in Learning and Professional Development*. London: RoutledgeFalmer Press.

Moos, L., Krejsler, J. and Kofod, K.K. (2008) 'Successful principals: telling or selling? On the importance of context for school leadership', *International Journal of School Leadership*, 11(4): 341–52.

Moyles, J. (2001) 'Passion, paradox and professionalism in early years education', *International Journal for Early Years Education*, 21(2): 81–95.

Moyles, J. (2006) *Effective Leadership and Management in the Early Years*. Maidenhead: Open University Press.

Muijs, D. and Harris, A. (2003) 'Teacher leadership – improvement through empowerment?', *Educational Management and Administration*, 31(4): 437–48.

Muijs, D., Aubrey, C., Harris, A. and Biggs, M. (2004) 'How do they manage? A review on leadership in early childhood', *Journal of Early Childhood Research*, 2(2): 157–69.

Munro, E. (2010) *Munro Review of Child Protection: DFE 00548–2010*. London: Department for Education.

National College for School Leadership (NCSL) (2004) 'Pioneering qualification supports joined-up children's services', NCSL press release, 24 May, available at: www.ncsl.org.uk/aboutus/pressrelease/college-pr-24052004.cfm, accessed 2011.

National College for School Leadership (NCSL) (2008) *Realising Leadership: Children's Centre Leaders in Action. The Impact of National Professional Qualification in Integrated Centre Leadership (NPQICL) on Children's Centre Leaders and their Practice*. Nottingham: NCSL.

National College for School and Children's Services Leaders (NC) (2010) *National Professional Qualification in Integrated Centre Leadership (NPQICL) Programme*. Nottingham: NC.

National College for School and Children's Services Leaders (NC) (2012) 'Presentation policy update', NPQICL Providers Meeting, 25 October, National College, Nottingham.

Neugebauer, B. and Neugebauer, R. (eds) (1998) *The Art of Leadership: Managing Early Childhood Organisations*. Vol. 2. Perth: Child Care Information Exchange.

Nutbrown, C. (2011) 'Nutbrown Review: mapping the early education and childcare workforce – a background paper', November, Department for Education.

Nutbrown, C. (2012) *Foundations for Quality: The Independent Review of Early Education and Childcare Qualifications. Final Report*. June. London: DfE.

Nutbrown, C. (2013) *Shaking the Foundations of Quality? Why 'Childcare' Policy Must Not Lead to Poor-quality Early Education and Care (March 2013)*. Sheffield: University of Sheffield.

Nutbrown, C., Hannon, P. and Morgan, A. (2005) *Early Literacy Work with Families: Policy, Practice and Research*. London: Sage.

Oberhuemer, P. (2005) 'Conceptualising the early childhood pedagogue: policy approaches and issues of professionalism', *European Early Childhood Education Research Journal*, 9: 57–72.

Oberhuemer, P., Schreyer, I. and Neuman, M.J. (2010) *Professionals in Early Childhood Education and Care Systems: European Profiles and Perspectives*. Opladen and Farmington Hills, MI: Barbara Budrich.

Office for Standards in Education (Ofsted) (2003) *Leadership and Management: What Inspection Tells Us*. HMI 1646. London: The Stationery Office.

Office for Standards in Education (Ofsted) (2012) *The Framework for Schools Inspection*. London: The Stationery Office.

Osgood, J. (2004) 'Time to get down to business? The responses of early years practitioners to entrepreneurial approaches to professionalism', *Journal of Early Childhood Research*, 2(1): 5–24.

Osgood, J. (2006) 'Professionalism and performativity: the feminist challenge facing early years practitioners', *Early Years: An International Journal of Research and Development*, 26(2): 187–99.

Osgood, J. (2011) 'Contested constructions of professionalism within the nursery', in L. Miller and C. Cable (eds), *Professionalisation, Leadership and Management in the Early Years*. London: Sage. pp.107–28.

Paige-Smith, A. and Craft, A. (2011) *Developing Reflective Practice in the Early Years*. 2nd edn. Maidenhead: Open University Press.

Parry, K.W. (2011) 'Leadership and organisation theory', in A. Bryman, D. Collinson, D. Grint, B. Jackson and M. Uhl-Bien (eds), *The Sage Handbook of Leadership*. London: Sage. pp. 54–70.

Pen Green (2012) *Early Years Teaching Centre Progress Report 2012*. Corby: Pen Green Research, Development and Training Base and Leadership Centre.

Petrie, P., Boddy, J., Cameron, C., Heptinstall, E., McQuail, S., Wigfall, S. and Wigfall, V. (2012) 'Pedagogy: a holistic, personal approach to work with children and young people across services', in L. Miller, R. Drury and C. Cable (eds), *Extending Professional Practice in the Early Years*. London: Sage. pp. 221–38.

Podsakoff, P.M., Mackenzie, S.B., Moorman, R.H. and Fetter, R. (1990) 'Transformational leader behaviours and their effects on followers' trust in leader, satisfaction, and organizational citizenship behaviours', *The Leadership Quarterly*, 1(2): 107–42.

Pugh, G. (2006) 'The policy agenda for early childhood services', in G. Pugh and B. Duffy (eds), *Contemporary Issues in the Early Years*. 4th edn. London: Sage. pp. 7–19.

Pugh, G. and Duffy, D. (eds) (2010) *Contemporary Issues in the Early Years*. 5th edn. London: Sage.

Raelin, J. (2003) *Creating Leaderful Organisations*. San Francisco, CA, and London: Sage.

Reardon, D. (2009) *Achieving Early Years Professional Status*. London: Sage.

Reed, M. (2010) 'Children's centre and children's services?', in M. Reed and N. Canning (eds), *Reflective Practice in the Early Years*. London: Sage. pp. 99–112.

Reed, M. and Canning, N. (2012) *Implementing Quality Improvement and Change in the Early Years*. London: Sage.

Rodd, J. (2013) *Leadership in Early Childhood: The Pathway to Professionalism*. 3rd edn. Maidenhead: Open University Press.

Rogers, C. (1961) *On Becoming a Person*. Boston, MA: Houghton Mifflin.

Rose, J. and Rogers, S. (2012) *The Role of the Adult in Early Years Settings*. Maidenhead: Open University Press.

Ruch, G. (2003) *Reflective Practice in Contemporary Childcare Social Work*, www.hants.gov.uk, accessed 2003 in R. Parker-Rees, C. Leeson, J. Willan and J. Savage (eds), (2010) *Early Childhood Studies*. 3rd edn. Exeter: Learning Matters.

Runte, M. and Milles, A.J. (2006) 'Cold war, chilly climate: exploring the roots of gendered discourse in organizational management theory', in *Human Relations*, 1(5): 695–720.

Sammons, P., Hillman, J. and Mortimore, P. (1999) *Key Characteristics of Effective Schools: A Review of School Effectiveness Research*. London: Institute of Education.

Schon, D.A. (1983) *The Reflective Practitioner: How Professionals Think in Action*. New York: Basic Books.

Shakeshaft, C. (1987) *Women in Educational Administration*. Newbury Park, CA: Sage.

Sinclair, A. (2011) 'Being leaders: identities and identity work in leadership', in A. Bryman, D. Collinson, D. Grint, B. Jackson and M. Uhl-Bien (2011) *The Sage Handbook of Leadership*. London: Sage. pp. 508–17.

Siraj-Blatchford, I. (2009) 'Early childhood education (ECE)', in T. Maynard and N. Thomas (eds), *An Introduction to Early Childhood Studies*. 2nd edn. London: Sage. pp. 148–60.

Siraj-Blatchford, I. and Hallet, E. (2012) 'Draft national standards for leadership of SureStart children's centre services: for consultation', unpublished, National College and the Institute of Education, Nottingham and University of London.

Siraj-Blatchford, I. and Manni, L. (2007) *Effective Leadership in the Early Years Sector (The ELEYS Study)*. London: Institute of Education.

Siraj-Blatchford, I. and Wah Sum, C. (unpublished, 2013) *Understanding and Advancing Systems Leadership in the Early Years*. Nottingham: National College Teaching Agency.

Siraj-Blatchford, I., Clarke, K. and Needham, M. (eds) (2007) *The Team Around the Child*. Stoke-on-Trent: Trentham Books. pp. 105–19.

Siraj-Blatchford, I., Sylva, K., Muttock, S., Gilden, R. and Bell, D. (2002) *Researching Effective Pedagogy in the Early Years (REPEY)*. Report for DfES. London: HMSO.

Southworth, G. (2004) *Primary School Leadership in Context: Leading Small, Medium and Large Sized Schools*. London: RoutledgeFalmer.

Spillane, J., Halverson, R. and Diamond, J. (2004) 'Towards a theory of leadership practice: a distributed perspective', *Journal of Curriculum Studies*, 36(1): 3–34.

Starratt, R.J. (2003) *Centering Educational Administration: Cultivating Meaning, Community, Responsibility*. Mahwah, NJ: Lawrence Erlbaum Associates.

Stoll, L. (2013) 'Leading professional learning communities', in C. Wise, P. Bradshaw and M. Cartwright (eds), *Leading Professional Practice in Education*. London: Sage. pp. 225–39.

Sylva, K., Melhuish, E., Sammons, P., Siraj-Blatchford, I. and Taggart B (2004) *The Effective Provision of Pre-School Education (EPPE) Project: Final Report*. London: DfES/Institute of Education, University of London.

Sylva, K., Melhuish, E., Sammons, P., Siraj-Blatchford, I. and Taggart, B. (2010) *Early Childhood Matters*. London: Sage.

Taggart, G. (2011) 'Don't we care? The ethics and emotional labour of early years professionalism', *Early Years: An International Journal of Research and Development*, 31(1): pp. 85–95.

Tarrant, J. (2000) 'Preparing for educare: student perspectives on early years training in Northern Ireland', *International Journal of Early Years Education*, 17(3): 222.

Teaching Development Agency (TDA) (2008) 'Introduction', in P. Earley and V. Porritt (eds), *Effective Practices in Continuing Professional Development.* London: Institute of Education, University of London. pp. 2–17.

Tickell, C. (2011) *The Early Years: Foundations for Life, Health and Learning.* (Tickell Review.) London: Her Majesty's Government.

Van Knippenberg, D. and Hogg, M.A. (2003) 'A social identity model of leadership effectiveness in organizations', in B. Staw and R.M. Kramer (eds), *Research in Organisational Behaviour.* Greenwich, CT: JAI Press: 245–97.

Vincent, C. (2012) *Parenting: Responsibilities, Risks and Respect: An Inaugural Professional Lecture.* Professorial Lecture Series. London: Institute of Education, University of London.

Vincent, C. and Braun, A. (2010) '"And hairdressers are quite seedy ..." the moral worth of childcare training', *Contemporary Issues in Early Childhood*, 11(2): 203–14.

Wallace, M. (2001) 'Sharing leadership of schools through teamwork: a justifiable risk?', *Educational Management and Administration*, 29(2): 153–67.

Weber, M. (1968) 'Economy and society: an outline of interpretative society', in A. Marturano and J. Gosling (eds) (2008) *Leadership: the Key Concepts.* London: Routledge.

Wenger, E. (1998) *Communities of Practice, Learning, Meaning, Identity.* New York: Cambridge University Press.

Weyer, B. (2007) 'Twenty years later: explaining the persistence of the glass ceiling for women leaders', in *Women and Management Review*, 2(6): 482–96.

Whalley, M. (2005) 'Developing leadership approaches for early years settings: leading together', PowerPoint presentation available at: www.ncsl.org.uk. accessed 2005.

Whalley, M. and Pen Green Team (2008) *Involving Parents in their Children's Learning.* 2nd edn. London: Paul Chapman Publishing.

Whalley, M.E. (2011a) *Leading Practice in Early Years Settings.* 2nd edn. Exeter: Learning Matters.

Whalley, M.E. (2011b) 'Leading and managing in the early years', in L. Miller and C. Cable (eds), *Professionalization, Leadership and Management in the Early Years.* London: Sage. pp. 13–28.

Wigfall, V. and Moss, P. (2001) *More than the Sum of Its Parts? A Study of a Multi-agency Child Care Network.* London: Cassell.

Wolfendale, S. (1992) *Empowering Parents and Teachers Working for Children.* London: Cassell.

Woodrow, C. and Busch, G. (2008) 'Repositioning early childhood leadership in action and activism', *European Early Childhood Education Research Journal*, 16(1): 83–93.

Woods, P.A., Bennett, N., Harvey, J.A. and Wise, C. (2005) 'Variabilities and dualities in distributed leadership: findings from a systematic literature review', *Educational Management and Administration and Leadership*, 32(4): 439–57.

Yin, R.K. (2003) *Case Study Research: Design and Methods.* London: Sage.

Yukl, G.A. (1999) 'An evaluation of conceptual weaknesses in transformational and charismatic leadership theories', *The Leadership Quarterly*, 10(2): 285–305.

Yukl, G.A. (2002) *Leadership in Organisations.* 5th edn. Upper Saddle River, NJ: Prentice Hall.

Index